IMMERSION
Bible Studies

1 & 2 CORINTHIANS

Praise for IMMERSION

"IMMERSION BIBLE STUDIES is a powerful tool in helping readers to hear God speak through Scripture and to experience a deeper faith as a result."
Adam Hamilton, author of *24 Hours That Changed the World*

"This unique Bible study makes Scripture come alive for students. Through the study, students are invited to move beyond the head into the heart of faith."
Bishop Joseph W. Walker, author of *Love and Intimacy*

"If you're looking for a deeper knowledge and understanding of God's Word, you must dive into IMMERSION BIBLE STUDIES! Whether in a group setting or as an individual, you will experience God and his unconditional love for each of us in a whole new way."
Pete Wilson, founding and senior pastor of Cross Point Church

"This beautiful series helps readers become fluent in the words and thoughts of God, for purposes of illumination, strength building, and developing a closer walk with the One who loves us so."
Laurie Beth Jones, author of *Jesus, CEO* and *The Path*

"I highly commend to you IMMERSION BIBLE STUDIES, which tells us what the Bible teaches and how to apply it personally."
John Ed Mathison, author of *Treasures of the Transformed Life*

"The IMMERSION BIBLE STUDIES series is no less than a game changer. It ignites the purpose and power of Scripture by showing us how to do more than just know God or love God; it gives us the tools to love like God as well."
Shane Stanford, author of *You Can't Do Everything . . . So Do Something*

IMMERSION
Bible Studies
1 & 2 CORINTHIANS

James L. Evans

Abingdon Press

Nashville

1 & 2 CORINTHIANS
IMMERSION BIBLE STUDIES
by James L. Evans

Copyright © 2011 by Abingdon Press

Library of Congress Cataloging-in-Publication Data

Evans, James L., 1952–
   1 and 2 Corinthians / James L. Evans.
      p. cm. — (Immersion Bible studies)
   ISBN 978-1-4267-0987-6 (curriculum—printed/text plus-cover, adhesive - perfect binding : alk. paper)
   1. Bible. N.T. Corinthians—Textbooks. I. Title.
   BS2675.55.E93 2011
   227'.2007—dc22

                                                                        2011010752

Editor: Stan Purdum
Leader Guide Writer: Stan Purdum

11 12 13 14 15 16 17 18 19 20—10 9 8 7 6 5 4 3 2 1

Manufactured in the United States of America

Contents

REVIEW TEAM

IMMERSION BIBLE STUDIES

A fresh new look at the Bible, from beginning to end,
and what it means in your life.

Welcome to IMMERSION!

We've asked some of the leading Bible scholars, teachers, and pastors to help us with a new kind of Bible study. IMMERSION remains true to Scripture but always asks, "Where are you in your life? What do you struggle with? What makes you rejoice?" Then it helps you read the Scriptures to discover their deep, abiding truths. IMMERSION is about God and God's Word, and it is also about you—not just your thoughts, but your feelings and your faith.

In each study you will prayerfully read the Scripture and reflect on it. Then you will engage it in three ways:

Claim Your Story
Through stories and questions, think about your life, with its struggles and joys.

Enter the Bible Story
Explore Scripture and consider what God is saying to you.

Live the Story
Reflect on what you have discovered, and put it into practice in your life.

IMMERSION makes use of an exciting new translation of Scripture, the Common English Bible (CEB). The CEB and IMMERSION BIBLE STUDIES will offer adults:

- the emotional expectation to find the love of God
- the rational expectation to find the knowledge of God
- reliable, genuine, and credible power to transform lives
- clarity of language

Whether you are using the Common English Bible or another translation, IMMERSION BIBLE STUDIES will offer a refreshing plunge into God's Word, your life, and your life with God.

1.

Partnership in the Wisdom of God

1 Corinthians 1–4

Claim Your Story

"Who tells you who you are?"

The question was posed by a visiting preacher during a chapel service my freshman year in college. He went on to say, "Initially, it is your family that tells you who you are: son, daughter, brother, sister. Then you start school, and that institution enters your world: first-grader, second-grader, high-school graduate. The region of the world where you grow up also tells you who you are: Southerner, Easterner, Westerner, or American. Culture also chimes in: baby-boomer, middle-class, white-collar, blue-collar. Then you get a job or go into the military, and they tell you who you are.

"Then one day you join the church; and from that moment on, everything that you have been told about who you are becomes subject to a new authority. Everything we think about ourselves or know about who we are must be held up to the light of our new relationship in Christ. Ultimately, as followers of Jesus, if Jesus is in fact the center of our lives as he should be, it's the Lord who tells us who we are."

So, there are many voices telling you who you are; but which one are you listening to when claiming your identity?

Enter the Bible Story

Introduction

The 2000 film *Remember the Titans* tells the story of the members of a football team struggling with the new reality of desegregation in their school. In an effort to deal with the challenges the young men on the team

9

and people in the community are facing, the local school board hires Herman Boone, an African American, as head coach. Coach Boone works his players hard, not only to be good players individually but also to be true team players. The coach understands that unless there is unity on the team there will never be success on the field.

The apostle Paul, while never playing football, certainly understood the importance of unity. Our effectiveness as followers of Jesus is seriously hindered if we lack unity of purpose and identity. If anything of substance is going to be accomplished by the church, we must act together.

Paul also knew the danger of factions. Dividing ourselves up among competing loyalties, whether they be racial as it was for the Titans, or theological and sociological as it was for Paul's friends in Corinth, divisions mean defeat for the church. Paul's correspondence to the church in Corinth was his effort to bring unity and peace to a congregation wracked with factions and competing loyalties.

The City of Corinth

We should not be surprised that the church in Corinth was having difficulty with unity. The city of Corinth around the year A.D. 50 could be a case study in diversity. A bustling seaport teeming with people from around the world left an indelible mark on the city. This was no rural backwater town.

The urbanity of Corinth manifested itself in many ways, including great diversity in commerce. Paul was able to sustain himself, perhaps as a tentmaker (Acts 18:3), while establishing the church in Corinth. There was enough demand to support himself without any assistance from the new converts (2 Corinthians 11:7). The city also harbored pagan religions, some having been in operation in Corinth for centuries, which influenced the lives of the Corinthians. These deep-seated religions created one of Paul's major challenges in uniting the church around the worship of God in the name of Jesus.

However, these same challenges also became Paul's opportunities. There was a lively spiritual inquisitiveness in the ancient world, a hunger for a spiritual connection beyond this life. Paul's promise of a dawning new age would have appealed greatly to those who were seeking something better, something more satisfying than the repetitive offerings in the temples.

Paul's epistles to the church in Corinth reveal that he understood these matters clearly. He knew how the challenges and opportunities were stressing the Corinthian congregation, and he knew exactly what they needed to hear to get back on track.

The Three Letters to the Corinthians

The New Testament includes two letters to the Corinthian church, normally dubbed 1 and 2 Corinthians. However, it's likely that instead of having only two letters that there were actually three or more. For this study, we will assume that 1 Corinthians is an intact letter but that 2 Corinthians contains fragments of two other letters.

We will further assume that the current order of the letters in 2 Corinthians does not reflect the actual order in which the letters were written. Therefore, as we go through the study we will consider 1 Corinthians first, then move on to 2 Corinthians 10–13, and conclude the study with 2 Corinthians 1–9. We will explain this in more detail when we get to those sessions.

Letters in the Ancient World (1 Corinthians 1:1-9)

Letter-writing was a common practice in the ancient world; and Paul's first letter to the Corinthian church follows the usual pattern, except for his announcing the theme of his letter within the standard greeting. He gets to it in the first line: "From Paul, called by God's will to be an apostle of Jesus Christ" (1 Corinthians 1:1).

Throughout 1 Corinthians, Paul deals with problems in Corinth and responds to questions from members of the church. He called for unity of purpose and identity. He worked against factions. He reminded believers that they were "called to be God's people. / Together with all those who call upon the name of our Lord Jesus Christ in every place— / he's their Lord and ours!" (verse 2). Just as Paul was called to be an apostle, the Corinthians Christians were called by their faith to all other Christians.

By putting this idea at the beginning of the letter, Paul established a basis for encouraging unity. The Corinthians already had much in common with believers everywhere.

In the second and third letter to the Corinthians (our 2 Corinthians), we will learn that Paul was also being forced to defend the legitimacy of his status as an apostle. Opponents of Paul had come to Corinth to undermine his message and his standing. So, again, he began immediately by asserting his call to be an apostle.

Paul concluded his greeting with a prayer in which he gave thanks for the believers in Corinth. He touched on additional themes he would deal with later in the letter when he thanked God that his friends in Corinth weren't "missing any spiritual gift" (verse 7). Apparently, squabbling over who had the best gifts had created a contentious spirit in the Corinthian church.

The prayer concludes with a return to the theme of calling and the introduction of the idea of fellowship, or as the Common English Bible (CEB) translates it, "partnership" (Greek *koinonia*, verse 9). Paul left little doubt about his expectations for the health of the fellowship in Corinth. Part of their calling was to be in partnership with God's Son.

Naming the Divisions in the Church (1 Corinthians 1:10-17)

Paul launched into the heart of his message to the church. A group Paul called "Chloe's people" (1 Corinthians 1:11) had brought him troubling news about life in the church. We don't know who Chloe was, though most likely she was a key leader or a prominent member. However, her message about divisions in the church prompted a strong, though pastoral, reply from Paul.

The first cause of divisions seems to center on which preacher's version of the message about Jesus was the most effective. Groups in the Corinthian church had aligned themselves around certain individuals. There seems to have been a Paul group, an Apollos group, a Cephas group, and a Christ group (verse 12). What nuances of preaching caused factions to choose one preacher over another we don't know. What we do know from church history and practice is that it doesn't take much to splinter a group. The differences between the preachers could have been small and perhaps not even concerning content.

There is nothing quite as painful as church schisms. Many people have suffered through the agony of seeing their church divided, and church divisions have a long-lasting effect. The pain of forcefully dividing a church can stay with a person for a lifetime.

In an effort to close the fracture in the Corinthian congregation, Paul posed three rhetorical questions: "Has Christ been divided? Was Paul crucified for you, or were you baptized in Paul's name?" (verse 13).

Having posed these three questions, Paul proceeded to answer them in reverse order. First, Paul expressed thanks that he did not engage in extensive baptizing. In fact, he named only two people that he had baptized. Baptism was practiced widely in the ancient world and not just among Christians and Jews. Participating in the rite often occurred only after a lengthy orientation period and called for deep loyalty. Paul's point was that he baptized for loyalty to Christ, not to himself; he was not trying to start a religion in his own name.

About the Scripture

A Common Mind

The Greek word translated "partnership" in 1 Corinthians 1:9 is *koinonia*. The word is built on two words, which if translated literally would be "common mind." The rendering of the word as "partnership" in the CEB and "fellowship" in other versions makes perfect sense from this. To have genuine partnership/fellowship, we must share a common mind about what's important. Partnership doesn't mean everyone thinks exactly the same way; but on the central values of the group, we share a common mind, a common commitment. For Christians, that common mind rests in our commitment to Christ.

Christ the Power and Wisdom of God (1 Corinthians 1:18-31)

Paul answered the second question in more detail. In doing so, he moved toward the central solution to the problems in Corinth. At present, they were allowing the patterns of social life that existed prior to receiving Christ to dictate their behavior. In the competitive world of urban life, it was common to align with an orator or a politician or a local hero; but the new world created by the death and resurrection of Jesus called for a new way of being together in the world. The basis for that new way was the wisdom of God.

This remains the central challenge for Christians today. It's the question we started with: Who tells us who we are? If we are going to be Christians, then that entails being followers of Jesus. We don't tack Jesus onto a life we are already comfortable with, as if he were an accessory to our life. Following Jesus means he becomes our life.Paul challenged the conventional wisdom of the current age with devastating questions. "Where are the wise? Where are the legal experts? Where are today's debaters? Hasn't God made the wisdom of the world foolish?" (1 Corinthians 1:20).

For Paul, the foolishness of God—that which seems foolish to the world—was in fact great wisdom. The idea that a new world may be possible because someone died on a cross was not only foolishness (to the Greeks) but also a stumbling block to Jews.

However, this so-called foolishness is the heart of God's wisdom. The cross as the means of our salvation makes perfect sense because we are not strong; we are weak. "Look at your situation when you were called, brothers and sisters!" writes Paul. "By ordinary human standards not many were wise, not many were powerful, not many were from the upper class" (verse 26). God comes to the world in weakness, just like our own weakness, and saves us by means of the cross.

As Paul put it, "But God chose what the world considers foolish to shame the wise. God chose what the world considers weak to shame the strong. And God chose what the world considers low-class and low-life— what is considered to be nothing—to reduce what is considered to be something to nothing" (verses 27-28).

Paul's appeal to God's wisdom overrode the competitive spirit that pits one group of loyalists against another. A competitive spirit that asserts, "My gift is better than your gift" is silenced by the command, "The one who brags should brag in the Lord!" (verse 31).

Proclaiming Christ Crucified (1 Corinthians 2:1-5)

Having demolished any basis for competitive boasting, Paul refined his reflections on the cross of Christ and the wisdom of God. He also laid the foundation for refuting one of the claims of his opponents. In later sessions, we will discuss what Paul called "super-apostles" (2 Corinthians 11:5). Apparently, some critics claimed that Paul was not a true apostle because he was ineffective as a preacher (2 Corinthians 11:5-6).

However, Paul never claimed special abilities. "When I came to you, brothers and sisters, I didn't come preaching God's secrets to you like I was an expert in speech or wisdom" (1 Corinthians 2:1). Paul's message was simple and consistent, not just in Corinth but everywhere he preached. "I had made up my mind not to think about anything while I was with you except Jesus Christ, and to preach him as crucified" (verse 2).

Not that Paul preached without persuasive power. Though he may have shared in the weakness that he claimed for Corinthians, his message was powered by the Spirit. The faith born among the Corinthians was the result of the power of God working through Paul's limited abilities (verses 4-5).

Admitting our weaknesses and living with them is not easy, especially in our culture that highly values winning and success. In fact, our sense of ambition and competition may be our best tool for understanding the forces at work in the Corinthian congregation.

The Wisdom of God (1 Corinthians 2:6-16)

Paul's point about wisdom, not so subtly made, is that the powers that operate in this world, in fact, that run this world, are not guided by God's wisdom. God's wisdom is hidden from these powerbrokers. Paul's proof? Had the rulers of this world understood the wisdom of God, "they would never have crucified the Lord of glory!" (1 Corinthians 2:8).

So how do we appropriate this wisdom? According to Paul, the wisdom of God is a gift that comes to us from the Spirit. We cannot learn it; we can only receive it. In this sense, Paul was describing divine wisdom as part of the revelation of God given to us in the life and death of Jesus.

Paul then asked—rhetorically—how is it possible to know the wisdom of God if no one is going to teach us? Or in Paul's phrasing, "For who has known the mind of the Lord, who will advise him?" (verse 16). Paul's answer: "We have the mind of Christ" (verse 16), but what does that mean?

In the Letter to the Philippians, Paul encouraged ethical behavior with these words: "Adopt the attitude that was in Christ Jesus" (Philippians 2:5). Paul went on to describe how Jesus, though in a place of privilege, emptied himself, became a human being, and died on the cross. Because of this, God has exalted Jesus and given him a name that is above every name.

Many scholars believe Philippians 2:5-11 is actually an ancient hymn that Paul composed himself or knew from another source. It is entirely possible that Paul taught that hymn to his friends in Corinth. As they quarreled and bickered over status, Paul reminded them of Christ's example highlighted in the hymn by saying, "We have the mind of Christ." The similarity of the phrasing in the Corinthian letter compared to the Philippians usage is striking.

Across the Testaments

Crucifixion

Paul asserted that the preaching of the cross was foolishness to Greeks and a stumbling block for Jews. For the Greeks, the use of crucifixion as a form of punishment was well-known. However, it was only used against non-Roman citizens—and then only for the worst of the worst. Why would God elevate someone crucified to the level of universal Savior? The stumbling block for the Jews was Deuteronomy 21:23: "God's curse is on those who are hanged." Early on, many Jews found it difficult to accept the idea that Jesus could be the Messiah because he died a cursed death.

The Danger of Divisions (1 Corinthians 3)

Paul took on the third of the rhetorical questions he had been answering in reverse order. He began by explaining the connection between the divisions in the Corinthian church and God's wisdom. He told them, in so many words, that they were acting like children. Because the wisdom of God had not taken hold among them, they had resorted to the wisdom of the world. Instead of becoming mature and united around their common faith, they had chosen sides to have what amounted to a "my favorite preacher" contest (1 Corinthians 3:1-4).

Paul acknowledged that there were differences in abilities and maybe even differences in the content of the messages the Corinthians had heard. However, that did not mean that one preacher was right and another was wrong. Rather the differences pointed to different functions.

Paul, who founded the church, compared himself to a farmer whose job it was to plant the seed. Apollos, a preacher who came after Paul, added his own take on the gospel message. Paul compared him to one who watered the plants. With the combined efforts, God gave the harvest (verses 5-7).

Paul then shifted metaphors from farming to building to illustrate the positive significance of diversity. A building requires several parts, and one worker may not do all the work. Not all builders possess the same skill or work with the same materials. However, if the foundation is good, the building will be successful (verses 10-15).

In all of this, Paul continued to call for his friends in Corinth to embrace the wisdom of God. Fighting over who had the best preacher is the way the world works; it is not the way God's wisdom works (verses 18-23).

It is sad that even today many divisions in our churches have to do with quarrels over leadership. Churches in the grip of dysfunctional pastoral leadership, or leaders whose egos are placed ahead of the needs of the people, can face painful decisions.

The Ministry of the Apostles (4:1-13)

Paul reminded the Corinthian church that it was not their place to judge the work of God's servants. That was God's privilege. The role of the faithful is to take what has been given and strive to be good stewards of God's gifts (1 Corinthians 4:1-6). He also reminded them that they had been given much. In fact, he told them they were rich. Paul may have been speaking literally. As he contrasted the wealth of the Corinthians with the poverty present in the lives of God's servants, he may have been reflecting the reality of living in a prosperous urban setting versus the life of an itinerant servant of God (verses 8-13).

With a Parent's Heart (1 Corinthians 4:14-21)

This section concludes with Paul asserting his role as "father" and the believers in Corinth as his "loved children." He told them he was coming to see them and that he would like the visit to be pleasant. However, Paul warned, if matters were not resolved, he would not be afraid to invoke full apostolic authority.

Live the Story

Who tells you who you are? For Christians this is so much more than merely asking, "What would Jesus do?" The deeper questions are, "Do we know the mind of Christ?" and "How do you live in the wisdom of God?" Considering these questions may help you decide: Where do your loyalties lie? What consumes your time? What do you find yourself vigorously defending or ignoring? How do you balance the spirit of competition that exists in our culture with the need for partnership and cooperation in the church? How do we handle the challenges to unity and partnership that may arise in our communities of faith?

Paul challenged his friends in Corinth to base their lives on the wisdom of God. Even though this wisdom is not always affirmed or understood by the wisdom of the world, it is the wisdom that has brought Christ into the world. It is the wisdom that will ultimately fill our lives with purpose and meaning.

What do you need to do now to base your life more squarely on the wisdom of God and claim your identity as a follower of Jesus?

2.

Where the World Stops and the Church Begins

1 Corinthians 5–11

Claim Your Story

Take a look around the church sanctuary where you worship. How is it different from other public buildings you might enter? Is there sacred art? Is there unique architecture?

What about the content of worship inside your sanctuary? Are there unique qualities about it that are different from other public events you might attend?

Consider your behavior: Do you act differently during a service of worship from how you might act at a sporting event or at an entertainment function? How do you behave differently once you return home because of having been in church?

The answers to these questions help us to identify where the world stops and the church begins. What we see, hear, and do in worship, and as a result of worship, reflect the unique quality of our life of faith. Hopefully, those lines are not too blurred.

Enter the Bible Story

Sexual Immorality in the Church (1 Corinthians 5:1-13)

At the close of Chapter 4, Paul asserted his apostolic authority boldly (1 Corinthians 4:21). At the beginning of Chapter 5, he takes that authority to a new level of intensity. Paul accused the Corinthian church of

The Role of Satan

One role of Satan in the Old and New Testaments is of a force that clarifies faith. Humans must choose to give in or resist. As they resist they grow stronger. For example, in Job 1:6-12, the Satan figure met with the heavenly court. Then Satan was directed by God to test Job's character.

In the temptation of Jesus, the Satan figure functioned to help Jesus clarify his identity and purpose. In another New Testament passage, Jesus told Peter that "Satan has asserted the right to sift you all like wheat. However, I have prayed for you that your faith won't fail. When you have returned, strengthen your brothers and sisters" (Luke 22:31-32).

Paul's command to hand the offending man in Corinth over to Satan so that his spirit may be saved seems to reflect this wider biblical use of the Satan character (1 Corinthians 5:5). If the man continuedin his immorality, he would perish; but if repented, he could still be saved.

condoning a level of immorality "that isn't even heard of among the Gentiles" (5:1). Paul mentioned that a male member of the church was living in a sexual relationship with his stepmother.

The text does not specifically identify the woman as the accused man's stepmother. We come to this conclusion by noticing the language Paul used. The accused man was "having sex with his father's wife." This particular phrase appears to come directly from the Septuagint, the Greek translation of the Hebrew Bible. The phrase is found in Leviticus 18:7-8, which states the prohibition of a son marrying his "father's wife." A distinction is made between *mother* and *father's wife*, indicating that a subsequent marriage had taken place. Whether the father had died or divorced his subsequent wife was not stated, nor did it matter. A man marrying the wife of his father, whether the father was alive or not, was condemned by Judaism and Roman law.

The response of the Corinthian church to this situation was less than exemplary. Apparently, they had done nothing. Paul accused them of being proud of themselves (1 Corinthians 5:2). It is not clear whether Paul was referring to the overall demeanor of the church, the bickering over who had the best preacher or spiritual gifts, or whether they were arrogant about that particular situation.

Regardless, Paul did not mince words about what their response should have been. Given the outrageous immorality on display in the life of this member, the Corinthians should have been "upset" (verse 2) or they should have "mourned," as the New Revised Standard Version (NRSV) renders the underlying Greek word.

Paul directed the congregation to take action. Though he was absent from them, he was present in spirit. As such, the church needed to act as if he and Jesus were present (verse 4). Paul instructed the church to assemble and remove the accused man from the membership. They were to "hand this man over to Satan to destroy his human weakness so that his spirit might be saved on the day of the Lord" (verse 5).

Paul was not merely demonstrating a puritanical streak. He believed that a failure to live up to the high moral and ethical standards of the gospel would have a destructive effect on the church. He used the image of yeast to illustrate how unchecked immorality could affect the church. It only takes a little to go a long way (verse 6).

He called on the church to engage in a metaphorical feast where Christ as Paschal Lamb has been sacrificed. This language points to the Hebrew festival of Passover and the great story of God's saving power.

This becomes the ultimate hope of true fellowship. Paul envisioned our life together as an occasion for true joy and celebration—not boasting and certainly not mourning. However, this would only be possible so long as the church stayed true to the ideals it had been given (verses 7-8).

Paul concluded this section with a powerful call for his Corinthian friends to avoid anyone who committed sexual immorality. Not only should the faithful avoid immorality themselves, but they must also avoid anyone who practices such things. Paul's clarity about what constitutes sexual immorality is shared by most church members today. While Paul was of one mind, the church no longer is. People of strong faith have opposing views.

Paul's reasoning is clear and harkens back to his thoughts on God's wisdom from the previous session. If we do not distinguish ourselves from the world, then no one will be able to tell where the world stops and where the church begins. Nonetheless, the church is called and committed to be in ministry for and with all persons.

Not many churches actively and overtly deal with the sexual practices of church members. Most of the time it happens in passive ways with people simply not being asked to serve in leadership positions or quietly shunned in other ways. The church as a whole would be healthier and have a more vibrant witness in the world if loving and structured dialogue took place more often, with churches using trained professional to facilitate that dialogue and insure the continued well-being of members.

Lawsuits Among Believers (1 Corinthians 6:1-11)

As if one thing reminded Paul of another thing, he moved on to yet another example of Corinthians letting the world set the direction of the church. The issue was not moral, but legal. Apparently, the disputes among at least some of the Corinthians had gone beyond theology and spiritual gifts. Some members had found it necessary to resort to the civil courts to settle grievances among themselves.

Paul took great offense at this practice. He pointed to the destiny that Christians would have in the coming new age. Paul believed that at the end of the age, believers would sit in judgment of the world (1 Corinthians 6:1-2). If we will one day occupy such a lofty position, surely we can manage petty disputes among us now.

Paul called for a level of sacrifice that would demonstrate the true integrity of the church. Rather than submit matters to the court, which would tell the world that the church is no different from any other human institution, it would be better to suffer loss. Being defrauded, Paul wrote, is better than being defeated by the world (verses 7-8).

To remind the Corinthian believers of the important role they had as witnesses to God's goodness and grace, Paul referred to their former life and compiled a long list of sinful practices that God would ultimately judge and condemn (verse 10). That list describes "what some of you used to be" (verse 11), Paul wrote, but not anymore. He proclaimed almost in the tones of doxology that as believers "you were washed clean, you were made holy to God, and you were made right with God in the name of the Lord Jesus Christ and in the Spirit of our God" (verse 11).

Members of Christ (1 Corinthians 6:12-20)

The ancient pagan world, especially in an urban setting such as Corinth, had various views concerning sexual activity. The Greeks and the Romans seemed ambivalent concerning sex among adults, but Paul was adamantly opposed to believers engaging in sex outside of marriage. Some scholars believe that there may also have been sacred prostitutes from pagan temples involved.

Paul began his argument against sexual immorality by asserting his freedom. He told his friends that in Christ all things are lawful, but not all things are beneficial. "Don't you know that your bodies are parts of Christ?" Paul asked rhetorically. Thus, it is not right to take members of Christ and "make them a part of someone who is sleeping around" (verse 15).

Paul evoked the image of a temple of the Holy Spirit as a metaphor for how we should treat our bodies. "You have been bought and paid for," he reminded them, "so honor God with your body" (verse 20).

The larger learning from this text is that followers of Jesus belong to God. Thus everything we do should reflect that.

Marriage, Celibacy, Divorce, and Remarriage (1 Corinthians 7)

In addition to the problems Paul had been addressing, apparently there were also questions raised by the Corinthian congregation in the correspondence to Paul. One of those related to marriage and celibacy.

Sex is one of the most powerful forces that exists among human beings. It can be a powerful force for good, deepening the relationship between a husband and a wife; or it can be a destructive force, dividing people against one another.

Paul understood this and counseled the congregation in Corinth to practice celibacy—if they were able. We may pause at this advice and wonder why Paul would be anti-marriage. It appears that Paul believed that the new age was going to dawn in the near future (1 Corinthians 7:29). In his first letter to the Thessalonians, written not too long before this Corinthian letter, he said that we "will meet with the Lord in the air" (1 Thessalonians 4:17).

For Paul, preparing for the soon-to-come new age by embracing Christ as Lord was the most important work of the church. Consequently, distractions caused by the demands of marriage were of secondary importance.

Of course, Paul was a realist. He understood that not everyone could set their sexual needs aside. For those persons, he counseled faithful marriages. "Each man should have his own wife, and each woman should have her own husband" (1 Corinthians 7:2).

Regarding divorce, Paul had a word different from one the world might use. For the most part, among Jews living in Palestine, only the husband had the right to divorce his spouse. Outside of Judaism, husbands and wives could exercise the divorce option. Paul, however, called on those in the community of Christian faith to not exercise those options. Christians who are married should stay with their spouse, even if the spouse is not a Christian (verses 12-16), as long as the spouse is willing to remain in the marriage.

For us, two thousand years removed from Paul's sense of urgency about the new age, the call for celibacy seems strange. Because we have a more developed sense about God's plans for the future and the realization that the fulfillment of history could still be eons in the future, the notion that we not marry is difficult to apply. However, the call to live in marital fidelity still rings true. The fulfillment of history may be far off, but the expectation that we live an exemplary life in Christ remains the norm for the community of faith.

Meat Offered to Idols (1 Corinthians 8)

Paul expanded further on the nature of our freedom in Christ as he tackled yet another concern raised by the Corinthian congregation: meat offered to idols. In the Corinthian temples, pagans offered sacrifices to their deities much like the ones Jews offered to God in the Jerusalem Temple. However, the remaining meat from those pagan sacrifices was then put into the marketplace and sold.

Paul was adamant with all his converts that they give up worshiping pagan gods. However, some Corinthian Christians believed if they bought and ate meat offered to idols, even though they hadn't participated in the ritual, they were still, in effect, worshiping pagan gods.

Paul's solution grew out of the heart of his theology. While he acknowledged that Christians are free to do what they want, not everything they want contributes to the greater good. "But watch out or else this freedom of yours might be a problem for those who are weak," he said (1 Corinthians 8:9). In other words, it is better to deprive ourselves of our wants than to offend a weaker member of the community. This connects directly with Paul's understanding of Christ's ministry to us in that he became weak, like us, so that he could redeem us.

Paul stated emphatically, "This is why, if food causes the downfall of my brother or sister, I won't eat meat ever again" (verse 13).

We face the same sort of challenge in the modern world. As Christians, we are free to pursue all sorts of behaviors that pose no challenge to our faith in God. However, some behaviors may be viewed by new or immature Christians as inappropriate. Paul might ask us, rhetorically, "What is more important, for you to get what you want or to keep the church strong and unified?"

Privileges of an Apostle (1 Corinthians 9:1-18)

A persistent theme throughout the Corinthian correspondence is the question of Paul's authenticity as an apostle. We will have occasion to study this in depth when we get to 2 Corinthians. For now, however, note that because Paul was not part of the original Twelve and because his encounter with the risen Christ and commissioning as an apostle came after the Resurrection, some in the Jerusalem church questioned his credentials.

Paul, however, was adamant in his assertion of the same rights and privileges as any other person sent by the risen Christ to proclaim the gospel. "Am I not an apostle? Haven't I seen Jesus our Lord? Aren't you my work in the Lord?" (1 Corinthians 9:1).

Part of the issue of authenticity has to do with material support. As we noted earlier, Paul made it a practice never to take money from a congregation in its formation. However, after a community of faith came into existence, he expected them to help fund his mission to establish other churches. In other words, he would not take money while he was there but would take money while establishing a new work somewhere else.

"The Lord commanded that those who preach the gospel should get their living from the gospel," Paul noted (verse 14). However, he reminded the Corinthians that he never pressed that right. He believed his work had more integrity if he worked for free, supporting himself, rather than calling on the nascent community to provide for his needs (verse 18).

Discipline of Christian Freedom (1 Corinthians 9:19-27)

Undoubtedly, the Corinthians raised the issue of Christian freedom in their correspondence to Paul, so he returned to that theme and explained exactly how our freedom should be applied. Instead of asserting "freedom from" this or that restriction, Paul demonstrated how he was "free for."

For Paul, Christian freedom allowed him to be flexible. Since he was not bound by ritual regulation, he could become all things to all people. He could relate to Jews and non-Jews, meeting them on their own terms so that he might be able to win them to Christ.

The key is self-discipline. Freedom carries with it a huge responsibility to manage our behavior and our actions in an honorable fashion. Paul used the imagery of an athlete who trains rigorously to succeed in a sport. "I do this," Paul wrote, "to be sure that I myself won't be disqualified after preaching to others" (1 Corinthians 9:27).

The need for personal discipline is as urgent today as it ever has been. There are many distractions our world puts before us that can make it hard to maintain a faithful life. However, just as in any discipline, the more we practice, the better we become in staying on track.

Christian Freedom and Moral Obligation (1 Corinthians 10:1–11:1)

Paul summed up his view of Christian freedom by comparing the church to the people of Israel wandering in the wilderness. Even though the people of Israel had great spiritual resources, they failed to live up to God's expectations and suffered because of it.

Paul warned the Corinthians that they were facing the same sort of threat. He warned them that there were consequences for using their freedom inappropriately. Continuing involvement with pagan worship, sexual immorality, and simply failing to live up to the ideals of the Christian life are all forms of unfaithfulness to God.

"Everything is permitted," Paul affirmed, "but everything isn't beneficial" (1 Corinthians 10:23). That simple creed becomes the watchword for our life in the community of faith.

What are the things we can do that build up the community and advance the gospel, and what are the things we do that tear the community down? Paul concluded, "Follow my example, just like I follow Christ's" (11:1).

Questions Concerning Christian Worship (1 Corinthians 11:2-34)

The Corinthian church was also experiencing controversy around issues of worship decorum. Paul, once again, was concerned that the Christian community distinguished itself from pagan religious practices.

He first discussed proper dress. Pagan temples offered a variety of robed priests and priestesses. Paul's advice for women and men who would speak during worship services was that they present themselves modestly and with dignity.

We should not read these words as directions for the church for all time. It is not necessary today that women veil themselves; and Paul's explanation about why men should not cover their heads and women should reflects a viewpoint of his day, not ours. However, the principle at work is timely. We in the Christian community should distinguish ourselves from the world. Otherwise, what is our supposed advantage?

The other issue Paul confronted had to do with the celebration of the Lord's Supper. Apparently the sacred meal in Corinth had become an opportunity for the "haves" to show off their wealth at the expense of the "have-nots."

Paul warned that there were consequences for not "correctly understanding the body" (1 Corinthians 11:29). Paul was referring not to the body of Christ symbolized by the bread and the wine. Rather, Paul was talking about the nature of the church, the body of Christ in the world. Eat your feast at home, Paul advised, and eat the Lord's Supper in unity.

The Lord's Supper continues to be a powerful symbol of Christian unity. Whatever form we use to take the cup and bread, it remains a communal meal. We commune with God, of course, but we also commune together.

Live the Story

Paul's challenge is not easy. After all, we spend a lot more time in the world than we do in church. We live by the world's rules, and sometimes we have to use the world's schemes and methods simply to do our job or fulfill our role in the world. How are we supposed to resist being completely submerged in the values of the world when we are there most of the time?

Paul's answer: Remember to whom you belong, whose life has given you life. Paul also reminds us that even when you are not in church, you are part of the church in the world. Living a life of distinctive quality and faith bears witness to the reality of Christ in our life.

What is it about your world that conflicts with your faith? Do you find yourself tempted to step outside the values and virtues of the Christian life?

How do you practice spiritual discipline? Do you have role models or mentors to guide you and help hold you accountable?

Can you serve as a mentor or role model for someone else who may be struggling to know where the world ends and the church begins?

3.

The Gifts of the Spirit

1 Corinthians 12–14

Claim Your Story

Have you ever stood with a group of peers and shouted out in unison, "We're number one! We're number one!"?

There is nothing quite as exhilarating as a spirited competition. Whether it's football, baseball, hockey, soccer, or even just checkers—playing to be the best of the best can be energizing. It can also be a character builder. A spirited competition can sometimes develop personal strength and endurance.

Unfortunately, the spirit of competition does not necessarily translate into every endeavor in life. Sometimes we need to work with others in a spirit of cooperation, not competition. There are occasions when the energy that motivates a person to be the best at some activity, actually puts that person at odds with friends, co-workers, and colleagues. That is nowhere more true than in the community of faith.

In Corinth, Paul faced a congregation that in many ways had organized itself against itself in a spirit of competition. He knew that unless he found a way to unify them, they would not succeed in their calling. Where is disunity at work in your congregation? What role do you play in that?

Enter the Bible Story

Introduction

We've already noted that the Corinthian church was divided over the prominence of their favorite apostles and leaders. Different factions were devoted to different apostles and held them up as superior to others.

It also appears that certain members within the congregation were holding themselves up as superior—not in terms of superior office, as was the case with the apostles, but in terms of who had the best spiritual gift, the best talent for the Lord's work.

Paul employed great pastoral and rhetorical skill in helping the Corinthians gain a better perspective on the presence and role of the Holy Spirit and spiritual gifts at work in their midst. Paul developed a three-fold strategy that, if heeded, would bring unity of purpose and even unity of spirit to the troubled congregation.

First, he labored to quell the spirit of competition by arguing that all spiritual gifts are of equal value (1 Corinthians 12). Second, he carefully inserted a powerful poem about love in between his two arguments about gifts to make the point that love is the highest accomplishment (Chapter 13). Finally, he provided boundaries for what appears to be the centerpiece of the spiritual gift competition: speaking in tongues (Chapter 14).

About the Scripture

Spiritual Gifts

How are we to think about spiritual gifts? Most of the information we have comes from Paul. It is clear that Paul believed that the Spirit of God confers upon individuals the abilities needed for the church to function. Are these supernatural endowments, or are they talents and abilities inherent in various personalities? It is not necessary to take an either/or approach to this question. Persons who are gifted with strong organizational skills may have learned those skills in business or school. Persons who are gifted with public-speaking abilities may have had those skills developed in seminary or under the tutelage of a mentor. It is not necessary to regard the gifts of the Spirit as only those that come through some supernatural ordination. God has many ways to get gifted people into places of service.

The Gifts of the Spirit (1 Corinthians 12)

Paul affirmed the presence and authenticity of gifts within the congregation, varying abilities conferred on individuals by the Spirit of God that allow the church to function. He was certain that the Spirit was evident in the lives of the Corinthians, but he was careful to describe exactly how the Spirit works. The presence of the Spirit is not going to lead someone to say, "Jesus is cursed!" (1 Corinthians 12:3). The presence of the Holy Spirit and the function of gifts resulting from our relationship with God's Spirit will always be "for the common good" (verse 7). There are many gifts, Paul affirmed, and everyone is gifted; but there is only one Spirit.

The underlying theme here is not subtle. If there is one Spirit providing all these gifts, and all those gifts are to serve the common good, then there should be no divisions because of those gifts. From this understanding, Paul began to develop one of his best known and most quoted metaphors. He asserted the body of Christ, the church, "is just like the human body" (verse 12). All the parts of a body are still one body, even though the parts are many.

"We were all baptized by one Spirit," Paul wrote, "into one body, whether Jew or Greek, or slave or free (verse 13). Since we are one body, it is ludicrous to act as if any part is greater than the whole. Paul employed a bit of satire when he wrote, "If the foot says, 'I'm not part of the body because I'm not a hand,' does that mean it's not part of the body?" (verse 15). He continued to develop this argument using various body parts (verses 15-21).

The apostle concluded by making this critical point: Instead of some parts being more important because they do more, such as the head or the eyes, all of the parts are important. The whole body cannot function without all the parts. Making some parts more important than other parts is simply misguided. "Instead, the parts of the body that we think are the weakest are the most necessary" (verse 22).

This perspective was likely to shore up any in the Corinthian church who felt their gifts were less than adequate. It also set Paul up to make his principle assertion that not only are all gifts important but also that all gifts are essential.

Paul used the concept of honor to make his way toward the essential nature of all gifts. Just as with body parts, some are seen and some are not seen. However, some of the unseen parts are the most honorable. "God has put the body together," Paul wrote, "giving greater honor to the part with less honor so that there won't be division in the body and so the parts might have mutual concern for each other" (verses 24-25).

Having made his point, Paul named some of the gifts of the Spirit: "In the church, God has appointed first apostles, second prophets, third teachers, then miracles, then gifts of healing, the ability to help others, leadership skills, different kinds of tongues" (verse 28). Note that speaking in tongues is listed last.

It is human nature that we value more the gifts that seem most significant to the life of the church, for example, preaching and administration. However, if we apply Paul's logic, the gifts that are not readily visible are also important and are therefore just as essential as the so-called high-profile gifts.

Paul also is quick to point out that not everyone has the same gift and that we wouldn't want it that way. The diversity of gifts adds to the health of the church and reflects the diversity of human personality and ability.

This certainly continues to be true for us today. The discovery and employment of our spiritual gifts is essential to the life of a healthy congregation. If a church finds itself with only a few people doing everything while others are uninvolved, clearly all of our gifted people are not being included.

Still, while valuing every individual's gifts, Paul said there are some gifts that are greater that every Christian should strive to exercise. "Use your ambition," Paul wrote, "to try to get the greater gifts" (verse 31). We can almost feel the anticipation in the Corinthian congregation. If they were in fact as competitive as they seem, the suggestion that there are greater gifts to experience would have them on the edge of their seats as Paul's letter was being read.

This, of course, is the genius of Paul's approach. He was meeting them where they were, seeking to take their competitive nature and use it as a tool to move them to a more healthy and unified expression of their common life. He was about to reveal to them "an even better way" (verse 31). Paul knew that if the Corinthians would adopt this better way, the contention and competition would end.

The Primacy of Love (1 Corinthians 13)

When Paul listed some of the gifts of the Spirit in the previous chapter, he put speaking in tongues last. He may have been making the point that among the high-profile gifts, speaking in tongues is not as important as prophecy (a point he would make explicit in the next chapter). As Paul reflected on love as the "better way," however, he mentioned speaking in tongues first. This may signal that there was a contrast to be made between those who spoke in tongues and those who practiced love.

This poem is well-known and used in many ways today; but in the context of the competitive atmosphere in Corinth, Paul used it to demonstrate a deep understanding of human nature. The poem also demonstrates Paul's skill as a pastor. He didn't want to strip the Corinthians of their ambition and passion. These are qualities that can serve the gospel greatly. At the same time, however, he didn't want their ambition to tear the fellowship apart.

It is likely that Paul was calling upon themes that were at work among the Corinthians. There were likely some who were speaking in tongues and claiming this ability as proof of superior spirituality. There may have been some who were exercising the gift of prophecy and claiming this as a higher or a better gift. Still others may have been claiming to have deeper faith and thereby occupying the more prestigious place in the congregation. The practice of charitable giving, knowing mysteries—these may all have competed among the Corinthians for primacy. However, without love, Paul wrote, they were nothing.

Again, using great pastoral skill, Paul sketched out what love is and what love is not. We cannot help but marvel at Paul gently calling his

About the Scripture

Speaking in Tongues

The phenomenon of speaking in tongues in Corinth was not the same experience that took place on the Day of Pentecost in Acts 2. That miracle seems to have been a speaking event in which apostles spoke in known languages they had never learned, and people present who spoke those languages understood the message. The Corinthian practice seems to have been more of an unknown or heavenly language that required someone present with the gift of interpretation to tell the congregation what was being said.

friends in Corinth to stretch toward a better and deeper way of being together. In love, there is no place for jealously or impatience, bragging or being rude. Love seeks the best for the other; and when authentically present, love never fails.

The poem closes with an eloquent reminder of the transitory nature of many of the gifts being championed by the Corinthians. Knowledge, prophecy, speaking in tongues, doing powerful works—all of these eventually fail. Paul wrote that there are only three things that endure: faith, hope, and love; and the greatest of these is love.

Love continues to be our most potent resource for demonstrating the truth of the gospel. Nothing is more compelling, more persuasive, than genuine acts of love. It is truly, as Paul asserts, the most enduring gift.

Speaking in Tongues (1 Corinthians 14)

Having declared love the greatest of all attributes, Paul next encouraged his Corinthian friends to "pursue love, and use your ambition to try to get spiritual gifts but especially that you might prophesy" (1 Corinthians 14:1).

We move here into clearly what was the heart of the matter for Paul. While speaking in tongues can contribute to disunity of the church, the gift of prophecy contributes to its unity. Speaking in tongues advances the individual, where prophecy advances the entire congregation. Clearly, Paul wanted to discourage speaking in tongues while encouraging prophecy. It is not certain that Paul wanted tongues eliminated altogether as a feature of worship; but it is clear that if they occurred, he wanted the activity managed closely. Therefore, in an effort to control the ecstatic practice of speaking in tongues, Paul offered three tests:

The Test of Social Concern (verses 1-25). How does speaking in tongues help the congregation if no one knows what is being said? The result is that the tongue-speaker may claim some special spiritual status, but he or she is the only one to benefit. What happens in the worship service should benefit everyone. If there is no one present who can interpret the tongues message, then the tongue-speaker should keep silent. So,

What does Wesley say? or Luther?

said Paul, "in the church I'd rather speak five words in my right mind than speak thousands of words in a tongue so that I can teach others" (verse 19).

The Test of Self-control (verses 26-36). Paul realized that if everyone simply did whatever he or she wanted to do, there would be chaos in worship. No one would learn anything, and God certainly wouldn't be glorified. In the heated competitive atmosphere of the Corinthian church, everyone with a verbal gift—psalmist, prophet, singer and tongues-speaker—was competing. It was necessary for all those gifted people to control themselves so that everyone who had something to contribute would be able to do so.

Implied in this directive was the not-so-subtle message that those who couldn't or wouldn't control themselves were not contributing positively to the life of the church. They were placing their wants and needs ahead of everyone else's. This behavior is the very seed of divisions in church life and even schisms.

The Test of Decency and Order (verses 37-40). Paul believed that the service of worship should have a certain decorum, a certain solemnity, that focuses on God and not on individual worshipers. He had already advised this group about appropriate dress in worship (11:2-16) and chastised them for their conduct during the Lord's Supper (11:17-34). The same sort of clamoring to impress seemed to be at work in the rest of the service as well.

Paul didn't pull any punches, even while trying to be pastoral. To all those who were so eager to speak that they disrupted the service, Paul asked pointedly, "Did the word of God originate with you? Has it come only to you?" (14:36).

Paul did not want to quench genuine passion. He certainly didn't want to hinder whatever legitimate prophecy may have come through the Corinthian congregation. At the same time, however, he knew that where there was chaotic competition there would not be meaningful communication. "Everything," Paul wrote, "should be done with dignity and in proper order" (verse 40).

Across the Testaments

Prophecy

The popular notion about prophecy is that it predicts the future. While there were prophets in the Old Testament who were able to foretell how events in the life of Israel were unfolding, the future was not their main concern. To prophesy meant to "speak forth." The prophets were those who had "a word from the Lord" about what has happening in the present.

There were generally two groups of prophets: those that were connected to the king or the Temple, and thereby were "official" prophets. We might view these in the same way we do advisers to political leaders today. Isaiah, Jeremiah, and Ezekiel were all official prophets to some degree. Other groups of prophets were itinerant or unofficial prophets. Amos famously falls into this group with his thundering, "I am no prophet, nor a prophet's son; but I am a herdsman" (7:14, NRSV). What they all had in common was an intense relationship with God and a sense of God's vision for the people of God that they translated into powerful poetry.

Prophecy in the New Testament functioned differently. Rather than being possessed by a powerful word of God, New Testament prophets were intensely involved with the Spirit of Christ. They were viewed as actually speaking the words of Jesus to the church. As the church moved through history, these prophets kept alive a sense of the presence of the risen Christ in the church. This was the gift Paul longed for his Corinthian friends to pursue.[1]

glad worship has become what we have!

This was a delicate balancing act for Paul. Being careful not to discourage legitimate and healthy spiritual practice was important. On the other hand, reigning in big egos and correcting spiritual practices that served only to feed those egos was necessary to prevent damage to the fellowship and to worship. Paul didn't want to discourage the Corinthians' ambition for spiritual gifts; but at the same time, he knew that ambition had to be channeled into practices and behaviors that served the greater good.

It's the balancing act all church leaders have faced throughout the history of the church, and it continues to be a challenge for us today. Obviously, there is great emotion involved in our relationship with God; but if that emotion runs ahead of our reason, chaos can prevail in worship. A balance of mind and heart will always be the best course.

Live the Story

If someone asked you what your spiritual gift is, how would you reply? Are you currently serving your church with your gift? As you look back over the partial list of gifts that Paul provided in 1 Corinthians 12, do you find yourself wishing you were able to perform any of these gifted activities? Do you feel a sense of calling in your life? In your experience of church, do you see others exercising their gifts? Are you able to see how these gifts contribute to the life and health of the church?

Have you been mentored by someone who you consider gifted? Have you mentored someone else? What was the outcome?

As we go through our life of faith, if Paul is right, God has provided everything the church needs to do its work in the world. Think about it for a moment. If Paul is right, then every congregation has within its ranks every sort of gifted person needed to do everything we have been called to do in the world.

Obviously, there are gifted people who are not serving for one reason or another. It is also true that there are people who are serving in places where their gifts don't fit. It is always the challenge of church leadership to cultivate gifts in others, help members discover their gifts, and then mentor and direct people into places of service that match those gifts.

Have you found your gift and your place in the life of the church? What can you do to identify your gift(s)? In what way can you make them available to your church?

---

[1]For additional information about this idea, see *New Testament Prophecy*, by David Hill (John Knox Press, 1979).

4.

Hope Really Does Float

1 Corinthians 15–16

Claim Your Story

What is the opposite of faith? Many would reply quickly by saying that the answer is doubt. However, while doubt is a common experience among all believers, it is not the opposite of faith. Sooner or later in the normal course of Christian practice, we are going to experience doubt about some aspect of our faith.

Usually, what provokes doubt in people of faith is personal growth. The faith that informs our life and beliefs when we are teenagers is generally not sufficient for our adult years. Our life as wage-earners, married people, parents, and individuals with grown-up responsibilities provokes personal growth. So do changes in how we think about and experience things. Sometimes, as we go through these different transitions, our faith comes up for review. We may find ourselves challenging beliefs we held when we were younger.

Pain and loss also provoke personal growth and changes in our faith. When we lose someone close to us, it is not uncommon to find ourselves asking, "Where is God when we need God?" Many people confronting grief situations find their faith strengthened as they move through the grief process. They come away with a deeper and more profound understanding of who God is and what God wants from us in the world. Some gain a larger perspective of the meaning of resurrection.

In this manner, doubt is not the opposite of faith. Doubt, as Saint Augustine wrote, is actually an element of faith. Doubt helps us to grow and advance in our understanding of the divine presence in the world. The opposite of faith is hopelessness, and in this session we will learn that one of the foundations for hope in this life is the promise of the resurrection.

Enter the Bible Story

Introduction

In 1 Corinthians 15, Paul discussed one of the most important elements of the Christian faith: the Resurrection—not only the reality of the resurrection of Jesus but the hope of resurrection for all believers. From the text, it does not appear that the Corinthians had asked Paul about the Resurrection. Rather, it seems he had heard about their questions and their doubts, perhaps from Chloe's people (1:11).

Chapter 15 falls into three sections, and Paul tackled a different aspect of their concerns in each one. In the first, Paul reminded the Corinthians of the historical tradition concerning Christ's resurrection (15:1-11). In the second, he addressed assertions that the Corinthians were making about the resurrection of the dead (verses 12-34). In the third, Paul took on two questions the Corinthians were apparently asking among themselves (verses 35-58). In Chapter 16, Paul talked about matters concerning the offering he was taking and closed the epistle with personal remarks.

The Historical Tradition (1 Corinthians 15:1-11)

Paul addressed whatever doubt about Christ's resurrection may have existed among the Corinthians by reminding them that there were witnesses to the Resurrection. "I passed on to you as most important what I also received: Christ died for our sins in line with the scriptures, he was buried, and rose on the third day in line with the scriptures" (1 Corinthians 15:3-4). He then enumerated the witnesses to the Resurrection, concluding, "and last of all he appeared to me, as if I was born at the wrong time" (verse 8).

Paul clearly hoped that this litany of witnesses would help answer the doubt of his Corinthian friends. It's hard to believe something someone else has seen or done, especially something so out of the ordinary as seeing someone who's been resurrected from the dead. However, the sheer weight of the evidence, the cast of significant characters, should have been a significant first step in addressing the Corinthians' uncertainty.

Across the Testaments

Resurrection

Although resurrection today is a central feature of Christianity and Judaism, the concept was late developing within Judaism. Most scholars believe that the notion of resurrection began to emerge within Judaism only after the Exile in 587 B.C. The only Old Testament reference that clearly points to a developed sense of resurrection is found in Daniel 12:1-2. Written around 168 B.C., these verses clearly reflect the Hellenistic influence on Jewish thinking. Even in Jesus' day, there was no universal acceptance of the idea. The Sadducees did not believe in a general resurrection. The apostle Paul used the disagreement on this issue between Pharisees and Sadducees to help himself during one of his many arrests (Acts 23:6-10).

The Importance of the Resurrection (1 Corinthians 15:12-19)

Then Paul appealed to reason. Apparently, he had heard that some in the Corinthian church were saying, "There's no resurrection of the dead" (1 Corinthians 15:12). This doubt was not so much about the resurrection of Jesus but about the general resurrection of all believers. We can be fairly certain of this meaning because of Paul's response: "If there's no resurrection of the dead, then Christ hasn't been raised either" (verse 13). Since Paul had just convincingly argued that Christ had been raised and that there were credible witnesses, then, said Paul, we can be sure he was.

The problem in Corinth may have been similar to one that developed in Thessalonica (1 Thessalonians 4:13–5:11). People in that church had become concerned that those who died before Jesus returned would not be part of the general resurrection. If some in Corinth had died and had not been raised immediately, as Jesus was, then that could have been the source of the doubt. Paul dealt with this issue in the next section.

The Order of Events (1 Corinthians 15:20-28)

Paul wrote that Jesus is the first "crop" of the resurrection (1 Corinthians 15:20). The general resurrection will not happen person by person. That great resurrection will happen at the end of a full process. Paul

Death in the Ancient World

In every culture, death is a persistent reality; but how people of different times and cultures view death varies widely. Apparently Hebrew thinkers only began to link resurrection with the reality of death after the exile in 587 B.C. For those who did not believe in resurrection, this life is the only life we have.

Among some Greeks influenced by the philosophy of Plato, there was a notion of the immortality of the soul. Plato believed that all matter, including human beings, originated in the realm of perfection. In each human is a spark of that perfect world, and at death that spark is set free to return.

Connected to views of death are always views of life. Many people in the ancient world lived stark and difficult lives. Life expectancy was short, and life itself included pain and distress. Only the wealthy were able to afford the sort of comforts that made life pleasant. For most, it was poverty and pain. Many scholars believe this is one reason Christianity spread so quickly and widely. The message of hope and life after death combined with the promise of an end to suffering were attractive to those whose lives were steeped in death every day.

described this event as the moment when "Christ hands over the kingdom to God the Father" (verse 24).

When we lose a loved one, the hope of eternal life and resurrection can be a great comfort, but usually not immediately. The initial response to the death of a loved is to want to reverse the circumstances immediately. That is why we often hear people say, "Oh, if I had only done this or that differently, this would not have happened." This is another way of saying, "I want this undone."

Only after a passing of time, after the initial shock and sense of loss begins to heal, can the promise of resurrection and reunion become a source of comfort and help. It is quite possible that someone in Corinth who lost a loved one remarked in pain, "There is no resurrection!"

Baptism for the Dead (1 Corinthians 15:29-34)

The expression "getting baptized for the dead" (1 Corinthians 15:29) is baffling. In the years following the first century, certain heretical groups practiced a literal baptism for deceased persons. They believed that even if deceased persons had not been baptized in life, they could receive the benefits of baptism for their eternal souls if loved ones were baptized as proxies for them. It is difficult to think that Paul would condone that.

An understanding more consistent with Paul's views elsewhere is to view the baptism for the dead as our own baptism. We are the ones who are dead and are being baptized in the hope of life. Compare this to what Paul wrote in Romans: "If we are united together in a death like his, we will also be united together in a resurrection like his" (Romans 6:5).

In other words, Paul pressed his point about the reality of resurrection by asking, "If it's not real, then why were we baptized? Why do we do the work of this ministry? Why am I risking my life if there is no hope?"

There's nothing quite as powerful as personal testimony. It may be possible to debunk an abstract idea with other abstract ideas. It is far more difficult to dispute someone who says, "This happened to me."

The Resurrection of the Body (1 Corinthians 15:35-58)

The third part of Paul's response to the Corinthian crisis of faith dealt with two questions the Corinthians apparently had been asking. Paul probably learned of these questions from the group that visited him, which he identified as "Chloe's people" (1 Corinthians 1:11). The first question was, "How are the dead raised?" and the second was, "What kind of body will they have when they come back?" (15:35). Paul answered the questions in reverse order.

Calling upon the world of agriculture, Paul compared the process of resurrection to planting a seed. He pressed the analogy pretty far, suggesting that when a seed is put into the ground, it "dies" (verse 36). Then it comes back, however, but in a different form. A seed goes in, but the full fruit comes back.

The human body will undergo a similar process, Paul asserted. "It's a physical body when it's put into the ground, but it's raised as a spiritual body" (verse 44).

The second question, "How are the dead raised?" is more difficult to get at. First, what is the question asking? Did the Corinthians want to know how resurrection was even possible, or were they asking how it was going to happen? The matter is further complicated for us by Paul's answer.

No matter which way we interpret the question, Paul didn't seem to answer it.

Instead, Paul talked about the defeat of death, our last enemy. He offered assurance that there will be a conclusion to this age, one that befits God's dream for our world. In other words, Paul seems to answer the question by pressing upon his friends the reality that some things are simply a mystery (verse 51).

Perhaps mystery is the best explanation we have. As we face life-and-death concerns and we deal with the real losses of loved ones, sometimes the best we can do is nudge people in the direction of hope. We don't know how to explain it. We don't have words for what God does for us after we die, but we believe with all our hearts that God will take care of us and that death is not the final word.

Alluding to Isaiah 25:8, Paul concluded, "Death has been swallowed up by a victory. / Where is your victory, Death? / Where is your sting, Death? . . . / Thanks be to God, who gives us this victory through our Lord Jesus Christ" (1 Corinthians 15:54b-55, 57).

Concluding Exhortation and Personal Matters (1 Corinthians 16)

In the closing section of the epistle, Paul took up two more questions apparently raised by the Corinthian church. The first was about an offering he was raising for the poor Christians of Jerusalem. The second was about Apollos, the gifted preacher at least one group in Corinth had claimed for themselves.

Collection for the Saints (1 Corinthians 16:1-4)

We learn from Paul's other letters that he had great hopes for the offering he was raising among Gentile churches. Not only would the money help relieve the suffering among Jewish Christians, but Paul hoped that the gesture would strengthen Jewish and Gentile Christian relations.

He provided careful directions for the handling of the offering. When the church met on Sunday, a portion for the offering was to be set aside for that purpose. In other words, the giving was to be done systematically.

When he arrived, he said, he would arrange to get the money to Jerusalem; and he indicated that he might take it there himself.

The raising of money in congregations can be tricky, especially if the money is going somewhere outside the church. It's always easier to fund projects related directly to the local church than it is for projects in someone else's church. Imagine, though, raising money for someone who does

About the Scripture

Paul's Offering for the Saints

Throughout much of Paul's missionary activity, he was preoccupied with collecting money for the impoverished Christians in Jerusalem. His commitment to this offering was reflected in several of his letters (Acts 24:17; Romans 15:24-33; 2 Corinthians 8-9; Galatians 2:10). Caring for the poor was part of the agreement he reached with Jerusalem Christian leaders when discussions were held about the status of Gentile Christians (Acts 15:19-21; Galatians 2:1-10). Paul's determination to collect this offering was motivated by authentic humanitarian concerns, but it's possible he had other motives as well. It's not hard to imagine that Paul longed for unity between Jewish and Gentile Christians. If that is true, then it is also not hard to imagine that his hopes for the offering would be to demonstrate to Jerusalem-based Christians the authentic faith of Gentile believers (Romans 15:27; 2 Corinthians 9:12; Galatians 2:7-10).

not particularly like you. Given the opposition to Paul in Corinth, he had set for himself a difficult task.

Plans for Travel (1 Corinthians 16:5-12)

Paul informed his friends of his plan to come to them in the near future and said he did not want his visit to be short. This may have signaled Paul's expectations that the problems he had addressed in the letter were to be taken care of before he arrived. This may have been behind the seemingly strange exhortation about Timothy. "If Timothy comes to you, be sure he has no reason to be afraid while he's with you, because he does the work of the Lord just like I do" (1 Corinthians 16:10).

Finally, Paul got around to the second question he mentioned at the beginning of this section: the question about Apollos. Apparently, some in the Corinthian church wanted Apollos to visit them; and Paul encouraged him to do so. However, perhaps sensing that his presence would add to what appeared to be a growing division among the Corinthians, Apollos had chosen not to go.

It is a mark of Christian maturity when leaders put the welfare of the church above their own egos. Had Apollos been a different sort of preacher, one easily swayed by flattery and praise, he might have decided to visit the Corinthian congregation. Given the fragile nature of the fellowship, as gleaned from Paul's comments, the presence of Apollos could have easily contributed to making a bad situation even worse.

Greetings and Benediction (1 Corinthians 16:13-24)

Paul closed his long epistle with a round of greetings and exhortations. This was standard form in ancient epistles; but Paul went beyond the usual format, as if he wanted to recap all the themes he had dealt with in the body of the letter. He wanted the Corinthians unified, and he wanted them focused on what matters. He wanted them to stop competing with one another and work together for greater good. Most of all, he wanted them to remain faithful to Christ.

"Stay awake, stand firm in your faith, be brave, be strong. Everything should be done in love," he says (1 Corinthians 16:13-14).

After mentioning several churches that are sending greetings, Paul put his finishing touch in the letter. "Here is my greeting my own handwriting—Paul." While he may have dictated the letter to a stenographer, he wrote that sentence with his own hand.

One of the marks of a good leader is the ability to confront inappropriate or immature behavior but to do so in a way that does not bruise or destroy the relationship. Paul demonstrated that he cared enough about his friends to confront them with their mistakes. However, he also demonstrated that he cared about them as his friends. That's good leadership.

Live the Story

There are many issues raised in these two chapters of 1 Corinthians that may have connections with our own faith. In our culture, we certainly understand the energy that comes from competition. We also understand the tendency to form cults of personality. We see that in the way throngs of people attach themselves to certain celebrities. We all have our moments of doubt.

Are there elements of the Christian story that you struggle with? Do you have doubt? Have you encountered the loss of a loved one and wondered where they are and if there is anyway we will ever see them again? Does Paul's explanation of resurrection help you in such times? How? In what ways can you use your doubts to grow in faith?

You may be in a position of leadership in your church or job. Do you have the courage to confront inappropriate or destructive behavior? In what ways can your faith help you to confront such persons in a healing manner?

In what ways does belief in resurrection animate the relationships and expressions of faith in your church? To what degree does it animate you?

We Christians say that we live by faith, and that is true. Sometimes that faith is tested, and we find out just how devoted we are to the movement of God we call Christianity. We need not fear our doubts. Doubts are just the soul's way of letting us know we need to grow.

5.

When a Tough but Truthful Word Is Needed

2 Corinthians 10–13

Claim Your Story

There's an old anecdote concerning President Harry S. Truman. As the story goes, he was speaking at a public event when he was interrupted by an enthusiastic supporter.

"Give 'em hell, Harry!" the supporter shouted.

President Truman grinned and said, "I'll just tell them the truth, and they will think it's hell."

If we wanted to translate that exchange to reflect Christian values, we need to do more than simply remove the profanity. We are charged by the very depths of Scripture to be truth-tellers in this world—not just telling the truth we have come to believe about God's love and the redemptive power of that love expressed in Jesus, but also to be truthful in our relationships.

That can be hard. Sometimes telling the truth becomes a matter of a painful confrontation. Occasionally we find ourselves having to confront loved ones whose behavior is inappropriate or destructive. Telling the truth is essential, but there are boundaries for Christians in their truth-telling.

To recast the Truman quote, we are charged to "give 'em love." If we do that, we tell the truth, even when it is hard; but the people we are confronting experience our truth-telling as love.

Enter the Bible Story

The Three-Letter Theory

In the opening session, we discussed the scholarly consensus that 1 and 2 Corinthians are actually at least three letters. First Corinthians is probably an intact letter, but 2 Corinthians is most likely the remnants of at least two other letters.

There also seems to be a problem with the order of the material in 2 Corinthians. The tone of Chapters 1–9 is joyful and filled with good tidings. The tone of Chapters 10–13 is more harsh, even bordering on angry sarcasm.

For example, in 2 Corinthians 7:16, Paul wrote, "I'm happy, because I can completely depend on you." However, in 12:20, he said, "I'm afraid that maybe when I come that you will be different from the way I want you to be."

Most scholars come to the fragment theory using what we know of Paul's travels and comments from the letters themselves. For example, from 1 Corinthians 16:1-12, we learn that Paul was planning a long visit with the Corinthian congregation to help with their internal problems and to collect the offering for the saints. In 2 Corinthians 1:15–2:2, he explained why he didn't follow through on that plan. Apparently, he paid a short visit that resulted in a painful confrontation that did not end well. Rather than risk another painful visit, Paul wrote a letter.

"I wrote to you in tears, with a very troubled and anxious heart," he said. "I didn't write to make you sad but so you would know the overwhelming love that I have for you" (2:4).

Many scholars believe that 2 Corinthians 10–13 is the remnant of this painful letter. They also believe that 2 Corinthians 1–9 was written after the painful letter, paving the way for the positive visit Paul wanted to make all along.

Therefore, for the purpose of this study, we will follow that scholarly consensus and begin with Chapters 10–13 in this session and conclude the study with Chapters 1–9 in the final session.

Paul Defends His Ministry (2 Corinthians 10)

There was something of a cloud over Paul's ministry. He admitted this himself in 1 Corinthians. In describing his experience of the risen Christ and his call to be an apostle, Paul wrote, "And last of all he appeared to me, as if I was born at the wrong time. I'm the least important of the apostles. I don't deserve to be called an apostle, because I harassed God's church" (1 Corinthians 15:8-19).

However undeserving Paul may have thought he was, he embraced his identity and purpose as an apostle with great tenacity. When his legitimacy as an apostle was challenged, as it apparently was in Corinth, he was prepared to defend himself vigorously.

Someone or some group in the Corinthian church challenged Paul's authority. Judging from Paul's responses, we can identify four basic criticisms.

The first was that while Paul talked tough in his letters, he was an ineffective speaker when actually present with the Corinthians (2 Corinthians 10:1, 10). Paul's response, in essence, was that he could be as tough and as strong as he needed to be, and would if he had to do so (verse 11).

The second criticism may have been aimed at Paul's motives concerning the offering he was collecting for the saints in Jerusalem. His anonymous critic(s) seem to have been accusing him of using "human methods" instead of relying on the power of God. Most likely, this charge was related to Paul's passion for the offering; but there was no direct explanation in the text for what the charge actually referred to. In any case, Paul responded vigorously that he fully understood the power of God working through his ministry (verses 2-6).

The third and fourth criticisms struck at the heart of Paul's status as an apostle. His opponents made the claim for themselves that they belonged to Christ (verse 7), with the accompanying assertion that Paul did not. Paul reacted strongly that he did in fact belong to Christ. The critics also seem to have been saying that Paul boasted in his authority too much. The underlying complaint here was that Paul had no authority to do the things he did (verse 8).

Paul took this last criticism on at some length. He justified his boasting with results. Of course, the results were not for his glory but for those who were receiving Christ. "It isn't the person who promotes himself or herself who is approved but the person whom the Lord commends" (verse 18). In other words, it's hard to argue with results. The many successes in Paul's missionary activity were for him vivid proof of the Lord's commendation.

We must tread lightly here. Paul is not giving us a blanket blessing to be braggarts. He was fighting for his apostolic life here and was forced to use the language being used against him to defend himself. As we go through life and find ourselves challenged at some point or other, it may be necessary to list our accomplishments as a way of defending ourselves. As a rule, however, humility in spiritual things is always the better way.

Paul's Assessment of the "Super Apostles" (2 Corinthians 11:1-15)

It is clear from Paul's remarks that there were internal and external critics undermining his authority as an apostle. He referred to individuals he called super-apostles as contributors to the discord in Corinth. It appears from his comments about these super-apostles that they were directly attacking Paul and his message (2 Corinthians 11:4-9).

These so-called super-apostles made specific charges against Paul: They challenged his authenticity as an apostle, calling him "second rate" (verse 5). They claimed he was uneducated and a poor public speaker (verse 6). Interestingly, they accused him of not taking money from the Corinthians for his ministry among them (verse 7).

We wonder why this would be seen as a negative behavior. In the ancient world, however, most itinerant philosophers and preachers expected audiences to pay for the performance. Thus, the underlying complaint about Paul was that his refusal to take money demonstrated that his message and his status as an apostle were deficient.

Paul defended each point strenuously, concluding that the super-apostles were the real posers. "Such people are false apostles and dishonest workers who disguise themselves as apostles of Christ" (verse 13).

Disputes that take place in church over or about church leaders are among the most painful experiences we can face. There are many people, who after a bitter conflict in their congregation, find it nearly impossible to be part of any church again. The leaders who are sometimes caught in the middle can also be severely damaged.

Paul felt that his mission and his status as an apostle were worth fighting for. We cannot help but wonder, between the super-apostles and Paul, how many people left the church in disgust or stayed but suffered deep inner pain quietly and for a long time. This still happens today. Simply because we tell the truth, even in love, does not mean people want to hear. However, when the truth is told without love, the reactions and ramifications can be even more harsh. For some reason, the pain inflicted in church disputes often leaves a deeper wound than other types of disagreements. Clearly, as Paul asserted, the stakes are much higher.

About the Scripture

Super-Apostles

There has been considerable speculation concerning the identity of these super-apostles. One school of thought identifies them as Jerusalem-based Christians, perhaps having a connection to James, the brother of Jesus (Galatians 2:11-12). Other scholars have identified them as gnostic Christians. Gnosticism was a virulent philosophy that denied the physical existence of Jesus, among other heresies (2 Corinthians 11:4). Whoever they were, they were not engaging in traditional missionary work, spreading their ideas as Paul and his colleagues were doing. Instead, they seemed to follow Paul around, upsetting and unsettling congregations already begun.

Paul's Apostolic Suffering (2 Corinthians 11:16-33)

It appears that the super-apostles were engaging in a bit of apostolic bragging, pointing to certain accomplishments or abilities that proved their superiority over Paul. So Paul decided to beat them at their own game. He acknowledged that his participation in this bragging contest was foolish (2 Corinthians 11:16-17). However, "since so many people are bragging based on human standards, that is how I'm going to brag too" (verse 18).

Apparently, the super-apostles had asserted that since they were Hebrews, they had the better grasp of Christ. Paul flatly refuted this by pointing out that he was also a Hebrew. He also argued that he had worked harder than the super-apostles. This may have been a dig at their practice of not starting their own work but of meddling in the established work of others.

Paul then enumerated how he had suffered for the sake of the gospel. He spent time in prison, was beaten, and he endured shipwrecks. Clearly, with the cross being the centerpiece of Paul's understanding of Jesus, his own encounters with suffering served to establish his authenticity as an apostle (verses 23-27).

The super-apostles also seem to have made much of Paul's "weaknesses" (verse 30). In Chapter 12, we will have an opportunity to consider what Paul called "a thorn in his body" (12:7), probably some kind of physical limitation or chronic illness. The super-apostles seemed to have seized upon whatever weakness this was as indication of Paul's lack of authenticity as an apostle.

We can marvel at the level of intensity with which Paul defended himself. What drives a person so hard to make sure his or her viewpoint wins the day? We might see such intensity as the defense of a person so insecure as to be unable to allow a single charge to go unchallenged.

Across the Testaments

Bragging, Boasting

In the matter of bragging or boasting, we can see how Paul's Hellenistic influence has helped shape him.

The Old Testament has straightforward pronouncements about bragging: "The LORD proclaims: / the learned should not boast / of their knowledge, / nor warriors boast of their might, / nor the rich boast of their wealth. / No, those who boast whould boast in this: / that they understand and know me. / I am the LORD who acts with kindnes, justice, / and righteousness in the world, / and I delight in these things, / declares the LORD" (Jeremiah 9:23-24; see also 1 Kings 20:11; Proverbs 27:2). Among the Old Testament Hebrews, it was considered a slap against God to boast, for in their view, all that was done was done by God.

Among the Greeks, however, this was not true. Greek historian Plutarch wrote a book titled *On Inoffensive Self-Praise* in which he argued that there are times when self-praise or boasting may advance a cause. When ideas are attacked or those who present ideas are slandered, self-praise is a valid defense. Paul seems to be following this precept in his dealings with the super-apostles in Corinth.

However, in the case of Paul, there is a better explanation. Paul believed the gospel of Jesus Christ is God's remedy for a broken world. If people will embrace its truth, the message of Christ's love will change their lives. Paul was not willing to let anyone distort or diminish that message, not even super-apostles.

Visions and Revelations of the Lord (2 Corinthians 12:1-13)

At this point in his defense, Paul claimed another sort of experience to legitimate his authenticity as an apostle. He acknowledged that he was weak, that he had "a thorn in his body" (2 Corinthians 12:7). It may be that this thorn was some sort of eye trouble, for Paul seemed to have dictated his letters rather than writing them himself.

Others have speculated that Paul suffered from malaria. His many travels would have taken him through disease-infested cities and swamps, and he easily could have contracted the disease.

The fact is, we don't know. What we do know is that Paul did not see his weakness as disqualifying him from being an apostle. Rather, he understood it as a reminder that God's grace is sufficient and that God's power could work through Paul's weakness (2 Corinthians 12:9).

Paul also used a different tack. Reverting to the third person—a typical Semitic practice when speaking of esoteric experiences—he talked about a man who was elevated to paradise where he saw and heard things ineffable (12:1-5). He was describing his own spiritual experiences and was perhaps suggesting that in them God had given him a special revelation into the meaning of Christ's coming. Paul intended the narration of these spiritual experiences to authenticate his message; it wasn't his bodily stature, but the stature of his soul vindicated his words.

Paul Anticipates a Third Visit to Corinth (2 Corinthians 12:14–13:10)

Having concluded his defense, Paul told the Corinthians that he was planning to visit them. This visit presumably was the visit that preceded the portion of 2 Corinthians we will consider in the next session.

Paul reaffirmed his decision not to be a financial burden on his friends. He also expressed openly his concern that if the matters he had been cautioning them about were not resolved, the visit would not be a pleasant one. He didn't want the visit to be about anger and rebuke; but unless there were changes, that was what they could expect.

Paul didn't mince words as he laid out his expectations for the pending visit. "When I was with you on my second visit, I already warned those who continued to sin. Now I am repeating that warning to all the rest of you while I'm at a safe distance: if I come again, I won't spare anyone" (2 Corinthians 13:2).

While these words sound threatening, Paul meant that no one who failed to follow his wisdom would be spared his wrath. He urged his friends to be introspective. "Examine yourselves to see if you are in the faith. Test yourselves. Don't you understand that Jesus Christ is in you?" (13:5).

These matters were important to Paul, and the church was important to him. He did not want them to fail. "We pray for this: that you will be made complete" (13:9).

It takes bold courage to tell the truth in love. Paul loved the people in Corinth so much that he would not let them go without a fight. People with intensity like Paul's can make us uncomfortable. The uncompromising desire to have things right can be unsettling. However, it is this kind of principled leadership that we need, not only in the church but in the world at large.

Farewell (2 Corinthians 13:11-13)

There is a sad poignancy in Paul's closing to this letter. Normally he was full of praise; he was effusive in his farewells and in his greetings. However, there was brevity in this closing that perhaps reveals his pain. This was a letter he did not want to write, for he felt bound to say things he knew would cause distress. He was hurt by the charges and criticisms laid against him, and he was disappointed that so many people whom he instructed were so easily lured into a conflicting version of the gospel. We get the sense he simply wanted to end the letter as quickly as possible.

Even in his hurt, disappointment, and righteous truth-telling, however, he couldn't let them go without a blessing. "The grace of the Lord Jesus Christ, the love of God, and the fellowship of the Holy Spirit be with you all" (2 Corinthians 13:13).

Live the Story

It takes great courage to confront someone in love. Have you ever felt the need to tell a friend or a loved one that they were not on a good path or that their behavior seemed to you to be unhealthy? Have you ever been confronted by someone who loves you and are concerned that your behavior is leading you down the wrong path?

Has anyone ever taken you aside and with great wisdom and affection cautioned you about your own behavior? How did that make you feel? Were you angry or were you grateful?

Obviously, how we are approached makes a difference; and not everyone carries the same significance for us. However, when someone whom we respect or admire, or simply have affection for, takes the time to confront us, in love, it is time to pay attention.

Where might loving truth-telling bring healing or help to a situation in your faith community? What might you do to help this to happen?

[1]From *The Interpreter's Dictionary of the Bible*, Volume 1 (Abingdon Press, 1962).

6.

Mending Our Relationships

2 Corinthians 1–9

Claim Your Story

In the complicated world of human relationships, nothing is more difficult than forgiveness. The Old Testament says that when God forgives our sins, they are forgotten; but it's usually not possible for us to forgive and forget. When we are subjected to outright betrayal, we might be able to forgive; but forgetting is unrealistic and unnecessary. There is nothing in the Christian obligation to forgive those who hurt us to also forget what they have done.

Forgiveness also does not necessarily require that we have an ongoing relationship with the offender. If someone hurts us and they do not repent of that hurt, we are under no obligation to stay in relationship with that person. The mending of relationships involves forgiveness but is actually about reconciliation.

Have you ever experienced the feelings of pain that come from an act of betrayal? Have you ever experienced what it is like for the person who hurt you to apologize and actively seek to restore the relationship? That is what reconciliation is about and—when it works—it can heal relationships between individuals and communities.

Enter the Bible Story

Greeting and Thanksgiving (2 Corinthians 1:1-11)

Scholars believe that 2 Corinthians 1–9 was actually written after Chapters 10–13. Those later chapters are probably a fragment of Paul's confrontational letter (2 Corinthians 2:3-4, 9; 7:8, 12). Based on what we find in Chapters 1–9, this painful letter had a positive effect. The problems Paul was so angry about seemed to be on the mend, and Paul was able to strike a more conciliatory tone in this letter. Having inflicted pain on his Corinthian brothers and sisters with a harsh letter, he was seeking to comfort them and work toward reconciliation.

Paul Sincere in His Actions (2 Corinthians 1:12–2:4)

First, Paul explained his reasons for postponing his planned visit to Corinth. One of the charges leveled against him was that he was inconsistent and unreliable as an apostolic leader. We looked at some of these charges in the previous session.

However, Paul made the case that postponing the visit was the best for all concerned. If he had gone angry and confronted those who were accusing him, there was a good chance that the matter would have escalated. The painful letter that he sent instead gave everyone a chance to reflect on the situation and work to solve the problems.

Treatment of the Offender (2Corinthians 2:5-11)

Paul turned his attention to the individual who had made the Corinthians sad and had hurt all the church members there "to some degree" (2 Corinthians 2:5). Apparently this person who had been at the center of the controversy had been dealt with harshly by the Corinthian congregation by "majority" decision (verse 6). We don't know what was actually done; but we do know in another instance, Paul had counseled that an unrepentant person be removed from the fellowship (1 Corinthians 5:5). Whether this was done with the offender in 2 Corinthians is not clear.

What is clear is Paul's expectation for dealing with that person going forward. He instructed the congregation to forgive and comfort the offender (2 Corinthians 2:7). It is worth noting the use of the word *comfort* here. Paul often started his letters with themes to be developed later in the letter. It is likely that even as he was beginning this correspondence, he was already thinking about how he would advise the Corinthians in their future dealings with this person.

Paul's insight into the dangers of not practicing forgiveness is worth noting. He told the Corinthians that the failure to forgive provides an opening for Satan (verse 11). Festering wounds in church life can grow into even larger disputes and disruptions. Better to resolve hurt feelings and reconcile members than to leave matters to get worse.

Thanksgiving for God's Leading (2 Corinthians 2:12-17)

Paul further explained his absence by noting other successes in his mission efforts. While worried because he couldn't find Titus in Troas, Paul nevertheless traveled on to Macedonia and launched new activities there.

The language he used is rich in Old Testament sacrificial imagery as Paul described his activities as having "the aroma of Christ's offering to God" (2 Corinthians 2:15), reminiscent of the sacrificial burning of incense (see, for example, Exodus 30:1-9). It is clear that Paul was pleased with the results of his efforts and therefore felt vindicated in his decision to postpone his visit to Corinth.

Across the Testaments

Covenants

Covenants have a long history in the ancient world. Outside the bonds of family, all relationships were governed by some sort of covenant. Covenants existed between ethnic social groups, tribes, and even nation-states. The most familiar covenant for us is the one instituted between God and the people of Israel. Mediated by Moses, the covenant we know in shorthand as the Ten Commandments established the rituals and ethical expectations that would keep Israel in good standing with God.

Over time, there were many breaches of the covenant by Israel. The Hebrew prophets interpreted the exile of the Jews that started in 587 b.c. as God's chastisement of Israel for their failure to keep covenant fidelity. Jeremiah was especially eager to have Israel regain and maintain covenant loyalty. He assured the people of Israel that God would not abandon them forever. God would bring them home, Jeremiah promised, and institute a new covenant with them. This new covenant would not be written on tablets of stone. Instead, the new covenant would be written on the human heart (Jeremiah 31:31-34).

For Christians, this promise was fulfilled in the ministry of Jesus. During the Last Supper, Jesus took the cup and told his disciples, "This is my blood of the covenant." Our use of the phrase *New Testament*, or *new covenant*, comes from this belief.

Ministries of the Old and New Covenants (2 Corinthians 3:1–4:6)

One of the charges leveled against Paul by his opponents in Corinth, and perhaps by the "super-apostles" who were helping stir things up, was that Paul had a tendency to brag and boast. Having just waxed eloquent about his efforts in Macedonia, Paul caught himself and asked, "Are we starting to commend ourselves again?" (2 Corinthians 3:1).

It also seems that the super-apostles came to Corinth bearing letters of recommendation, possibly from some of the "influential leaders" of the church in Jerusalem (Galatians 2:1-10). However, Paul wrote that he didn't need letters of recommendation. The believers in Corinth, their faith, and the work that he and others had done in their midst were all the "letters" of recommendation he needed.

Paul made clear that he took no credit for whatever had been accomplished through him. Whatever credibility, whatever success, whatever "qualification" (2 Corinthians 3:5), came from God. It was God who had made Paul and his colleagues "ministers of a new covenant" (verse 6).

Using the language of "new covenant" immediately caused Paul to reflect on the role of the previous covenant, encapsulated in the law of Moses. Paul alluded to certain legal requirements of that Law, primarily to the rituals of purity and the restrictions on foods. He referred to those laws as "the ministry that brought death" and were "carved in letters on stone tablets" (3:7). Paul often made contrasts between the old and new covenants; but given the context of criticism of his authority, this particular contrast took new depth. Paul was actually comparing his ministry to that of Moses.

Paul referred to Exodus 34:29-35, where Moses' face was described as shining because of being in the presence of God. This was such an unsettling sight for the people of Israel that Moses wore a veil when with the people but removed it in the presence of God.

Paul used this uncanny occurrence to make his point about the fading glory of the Law. Paul asserted that Moses continued to wear the veil long after the glow had faded. In the same way, the law of Moses was "veiled" from its readers, implying that its meaning wasn't clear (2 Corinthians 3:14-15).

Paul gave God all the credit
God made us who we are today — far from perfect
but not where we could be — —

However, because of the work of Christ, "all of us are looking with unveiled faces at the glory of the Lord" (verse 18). Paul insisted that the gospel he preached was not veiled; there was no deception in what he said or did. If it were veiled, it was only veiled to those who set themselves against the truth (4:3).

We may be a bit surprised that Paul would speak so boldly, aligning himself alongside the prophet of the Jewish law, Moses. However, he was careful to qualify his meaning: "We don't preach ourselves," Paul wrote. "Instead, we preach about Jesus as Lord, and we describe ourselves as your slaves for Jesus' sake" (4:5).

people: look at Paul
what did he do to cause
God to afflict him

Sufferings, Power, and Hope of an Apostle (2 Corinthians 4:7–5:10)

As we noted in Session 5, Paul was being criticized for his weakness. He had some sort of "thorn" in his body (1 Corinthians 12:7) that hindered him, and his opponents apparently used this to question his ministry and challenge his apostolic authority.

However, Paul didn't see his inherent weakness as evidence of his lack of legitimacy. To him, it proved the validity of his gospel of Jesus and the cross. Having just waxed eloquent about the glory found in the new covenant, a glory far better than Moses' fading glory, Paul put it in perspective with his suffering as an apostle: "But we have this treasure in clay pots." In other words, the new covenant, the new glory, is housed in human bodies; and human bodies are as fragile as clay pots. They can get sick, they can get hurt, and they can wear out; but that shows that the gospel power of which Paul and his co-workers were stewards comes from God, not from the humans that carry it.

Shifting metaphors from clay pots to tents, Paul wrote, "We know that if the tent that we live in on earth is torn down, we have a building from God. It's a house that isn't handmade, which is eternal and located in heaven" (2 Corinthians 5:1).

The fact that Paul suffered demonstrated his faithfulness to his ministry; it did not disqualify him or his message. For Paul, it served to validate the meaning of Jesus' death on the cross.

The Apostolic Gospel (2 Corinthians 5:11–6:2)

Having defended his ministry and answered charges concerning his weakness, Paul began stating conclusions about the nature of his message itself. He cast his work as "a ministry of reconciliation" (2 Corinthians 5:18).

For Paul, the problem humanity faces is separation from God's love. The death of Christ on the cross was an act of sacrificial love intended to bridge the gap between humanity and God. According to Paul, God was in Christ "reconciling the world to himself" (verse 19). As a result, Paul and other believers—including us who believe—have been reconciled to God through the work of Christ (verse 18).

Additionally, because we have been reconciled to God by the death of Jesus, we are now part of this great ministry of reconciliation. God has called us to be part of this great endeavor to bring humanity into an awareness of God's love for us.

Paul used the image of an ambassador to describe the work he and his co-workers did on Christ's behalf. "We beg you as Christ's representatives, 'Be reconciled to God!' " (verse 20). This work of being Christ's representatives is not merely the calling of a chosen few. Everyone who bears the name of Christ is called, in one form or another, to be ministers of reconciliation. We may not all have the same gifts for this calling, but we are called to contribute in some way to this central work of God in the world.

The Apostolic Life (2 Corinthians 6:3-10)

Paul returned to the theme of suffering for the sake of the gospel. Every negative and painful thing that Paul and his colleagues had endured had only served to "commend [themselves] as ministers of God in every way" (2 Corinthians 6:4). The list of Paul's sufferings is long and, if we are honest with ourselves, daunting. How many of us would be so committed to the Lord that we would endure the hardships detailed by Paul in verses 3-10? And not only endure, but also see these hardships as badges of faithfulness, proving our trustworthiness as ministers of God's hope for reconciliation?

Appeal for an Open Heart (2 Corinthians 6:11–7:4)

Paul made the implications for this ministry of reconciliation clear as he called for the Corinthian Christians to remove the "boundaries on [their] affection" for him and his co-workers (2 Corinthians 6:12). He encouraged them to "open [their] hearts wide," in the same way he had opened his heart to them (verses 11, 13). The key to reconciliation is for all parties to be honest with one another, so that they can move to forgiveness; ongoing communication; and, ultimately, trust.

The Joy of Reconciliation (2 Corinthians 7:5-16)

Paul returned to the theme of comfort that he laced into his initial greeting. When Titus finally caught up with Paul, he brought a good report: "We weren't comforted only by his arrival but also by the comfort he had received from you. He told us about your desire to see me, how you were sorry, and about your concern for me, so that I was even happier" (2 Corinthians 7:7).

If indeed Chapters 10–13 represent that earlier and painful letter, we can judge from Paul's remarks here that the letter had a good effect. Titus found the Corinthian congregation chastened and repentant. More importantly for Paul, the seeds of reconciliation appeared to be at work. He had already indicated his desire for the relationship to be healed. The report from Titus indicated that at least some in the Corinthian congregation were equally eager for the rift to be mended.

The Collection for Jerusalem (2 Corinthians 8–9)

With this reconciliation groundwork done, Paul was ready to regain momentum on the offering he was collecting for the saints in Jerusalem. It's not hard to imagine how important this offering was for Paul. Obviously, the offering fulfilled a pledge he made to the leaders in Jerusalem when his ministry to the Gentiles was confirmed (Galatians 2:10). However, there was likely more at stake for Paul than just relieving the suffering of the poor.

The very presence of the super-apostles seemed to indicate that Paul's ministry was still under a cloud and, by extension, the recognition by the church that Gentiles could become followers of Jesus without first embracing Judaism. We know that there were factions from Jerusalem that went to the Galatian church with demands that believers there be circumcised. It is possible that Paul's long recitation on the old and new covenants in this letter is partly addressed to those Jewish Christians who would have had believers observe at least some of the ritual laws of the old covenant.

So the offering could be viewed as Paul's way of seeking conciliation between Jewish and Gentile believers. A gesture of compassion that could lift the suspicion that Gentiles could be "real" Christians and create a unified church would fulfill a deep longing in Paul, the Jewish apostle to the Gentiles.

Paul made it clear that he was not ordering the Corinthians to make this offering. He wanted willing participation. "I'm not giving an order, but by mentioning the commitment of others, I'm trying to prove the authenticity of your love also" (2 Corinthians 8:8).

Paul also laid out a simple rationale for giving that has become the bedrock for church stewardship. Paul did not want the Corinthians to impoverish themselves at the expense of others. However, in the economy of God's grace, those who have are in a position to help those who do not have. "At the present moment, your surplus can fill their deficit so that in the future their surplus can fill your deficit. In this way there is equality" (8:14).

There are obvious concerns about handling large sums of money across great distances. Paul went out of his way to assure the Corinthians that every contingency had been considered. Titus, who apparently had gained respect and honor among the Corinthians, would be charged with collecting the money. Then he would travel with Paul to Jerusalem to deliver the offering.

The handling of money in the life of the church always calls for great integrity. Responsible leaders understand how quickly credibility can be damaged by poor stewardship. Having just begun the fragile business of reestablishing a loving relationship with the Corinthian church, the last thing Paul wanted to see was renewal of animosity because of money.

Paul closed the letter with words of kindness. He told the Corinthians how he talked about them in other places: "I brag about you to the Macedonians, saying, 'Greece has been ready since last year,' and your enthusiasm has motivated most of them" (9:2).

Paul again encouraged the Corinthians to give only as they felt they could, but he wanted them to be bold. Using a metaphor from farming, Paul said that planting only a few seeds yields only a small crop (9:6).

Paul assured the congregation that they could give boldly and without fear. God loved them and would make sure their needs were met. It was not that they could give and expect God to reward them with wealth. It was more a matter of not being afraid to give out of fear that they would become poor (9:10).

Paul also believed that the gift would result in the people of God giving honor to God (9:13).

In what might be the clearest statement of Paul's hope that the gift would help bring conciliation between Jewish and Gentile Christians, Paul wrote, "They will also pray for you, and they will care deeply for you because of the outstanding grace that God has given you" (9:14).

For a minister who feels called to a ministry of reconciliation, this is a great hope. To unify the church and to consolidate its resources for the work of the gospel was likely Paul's ultimate goal. When a congregation seeks reconciliation between the world and God, it embraces a life-giving identity. Individual members are able to use whatever talents they possess to contribute to this work. A ministry of reconciliation becomes a unifying, identity-producing, and life-giving experience for every member.

Live the Story

Where does your passion in life come from? What is it that gets your energy fired up? Is it sports or some other hobby? Is it your career or relationships?

Do you sense that you have a calling in life? Perhaps you don't feel called to a career to ordained ministry; but do you feel called to the ministry God offers in family, work, and world?

Are you aware of people or groups within your sphere of influence for whom reconciliation is needed? Is there a role you can play to help bring that reconciliation about? What is your first step? When will you take it?

Is there someone in your life with whom you need to seek reconciliation? We began this session talking about forgiveness, and obviously that's the first step; but what about the next step? Is there someone you need to call? When will you do it?

Not all forgiveness leads to reconciliation, and not all relationship breaches are reconcilable. In the ones that are, however, reconciliation usually should be attempted.

Paul argued that reconciliation can lead to a greater unity in the church family, which in turn can lead to greater glory for God. Few things in life are more important than that.

Leader Guide

People often view the Bible as a maze of obscure people, places, and events from centuries ago and struggle to relate it to their daily lives. IMMERSION invites us to experience the Bible as a record of God's loving revelation to humankind. These studies recognize our emotional, spiritual, and intellectual needs and welcome us into the Bible story and into deeper faith.

As leader of an IMMERSION group, you will help participants to encounter the Word of God and the God of the Word that will lead to new creation in Christ. You do not have to be an expert to lead; in fact, you will participate with your group in listening to and applying God's life-transforming Word to your lives. You and your group will explore the building blocks of the Christian faith through key stories, people, ideas, and teachings in every book of the Bible. You will also explore the bridges and points of connection between the Old and New Testaments.

Choosing and Using the Bible

The central goal of IMMERSION is engaging the members of your group with the Bible in a way that informs their minds, forms their hearts, and transforms the way they live out their Christian faith. Participants will need this study book and a Bible. IMMERSION is an excellent accompaniment to the Common English Bible (CEB). It shares with the CEB four common aims: clarity of language, faith in the Bible's power to transform lives, the emotional expectation that people will find the love of God, and the rational expectation that people will find the knowledge of God.

Other recommended study Bibles include *The New Interpreter's Study Bible* (NRSV), *The New Oxford Annotated Study Bible* (NRSV), *The HarperCollins Study Bible* (NRSV), the NIV and TNIV Study Bibles, and the *Archaeological Study Bible* (NIV). Encourage participants to use more than one translation. *The Message: The Bible in Contemporary Language* is a modern paraphrase of the Bible, based on the original languages. Eugene H. Peterson has created a masterful presentation of the Scripture text, which is best used alongside rather than in place of the CEB or another primary English translation.

One of the most reliable interpreters of the Bible's meaning is the Bible itself. Invite participants first of all to allow Scripture to have its say. Pay attention to context. Ask questions of the text. Read every passage with curiosity, always seeking to answer the basic Who?

What? Where? When? and Why? questions.

Bible study groups should also have handy essential reference resources in case someone wants more information or needs clarification on specific words, terms, concepts, places, or people mentioned in the Bible. A Bible dictionary, Bible atlas, concordance, and one-volume Bible commentary together make for a good, basic reference library.

The Leader's Role

An effective leader prepares ahead. This leader guide provides easy to follow, step-by-step suggestions for leading a group. The key task of the leader is to guide discussion and activities that will engage heart and head and will invite faith development. Discussion questions are included, and you may want to add questions posed by you or your group. Here are suggestions for helping your group engage Scripture:

State questions clearly and simply.

Ask questions that move Bible truths from "outside" (dealing with concepts, ideas, or information about a passage) to "inside" (relating to the experiences, hopes, and dreams of the participants).

Work for variety in your questions, including compare and contrast, information recall, motivation, connections, speculation, and evaluation.

Avoid questions that call for yes-or-no responses or answers that are obvious.

Don't be afraid of silence during a discussion. It often yields especially thoughtful comments.

Test questions before using them by attempting to answer them yourself.

When leading a discussion, pay attention to the mood of your group by "listening" with your eyes as well as your ears.

Guidelines for the Group

IMMERSION is designed to promote full engagement with the Bible for the purpose of growing faith and building up Christian community. While much can be gained from individual reading, a group Bible study offers an ideal setting in which to achieve these aims. Encourage participants to bring their Bibles and read from Scripture during the session. Invite participants to consider the following guidelines as they participate in the group:

Respect differences of interpretation and understanding.

Support one another with Christian kindness, compassion, and courtesy.

Listen to others with the goal of understanding rather than agreeing or disagreeing.

Celebrate the opportunity to grow in faith through Bible study.

Approach the Bible as a dialogue partner, open to the possibility of being challenged or changed by God's Word.

Recognize that each person brings unique and valuable life experiences to the group and is an important part of the community.

Reflect theologically—that is, be attentive to three basic questions: What does this say about God? What does this say about me/us? What does this say about the relationship between God and me/us?

Commit to a *lived faith response* in light of insights you gain from the Bible. In other words, what changes in attitudes (how you believe) or actions (how you behave) are called for by God's Word?

Group Sessions

The group sessions, like the chapters themselves, are built around three sections: "Claim Your Story," "Enter the Bible Story," and "Live the Story." Sessions are designed to move participants from an awareness of their own life story, issues, needs, and experiences into an encounter and dialogue with the story of Scripture and to make decisions integrating their personal stories and the Bible's story.

The session plans in the following pages will provide questions and activities to help your group focus on the particular content of each chapter. In addition to questions and activities, the plans will include chapter title, Scripture, and faith focus.

Here are things to keep in mind for all the sessions:

Prepare Ahead

Study the Scripture, comparing different translations and perhaps a paraphrase.

Read the chapter, and consider what it says about your life and the Scripture.

Gather materials such as large sheets of paper or a markerboard with markers.

Prepare the learning area. Write the faith focus for all to see.

Welcome Participants

Invite participants to greet one another.

Tell them to find one or two people and talk about the faith focus.

Ask: What words stand out for you? Why?

Guide the Session

Look together at "Claim Your Story." Ask participants to give their reactions to the stories and examples given in each chapter. Use questions from the session plan to elicit comments based on personal experiences and insights.

Ask participants to open their Bibles and "Enter the Bible Story." For each portion of Scripture, use questions from the session plan to help participants gain insight into the text and relate it to issues in their lives.

Step through the activity or questions posed in "Live the Story." Encourage participants to embrace what they have learned and apply it in their daily lives.

Invite participants to offer their responses or insights about the boxed material in "Across the Testaments," "About the Scripture," and "About the Christian Faith."

Close the Session

Encourage participants to read the following week's Scripture and chapter before the next session.

Offer a closing prayer.

1. Partnership in the Wisdom of God

1 Corinthians 1–4

Faith Focus

The wisdom of God, embodied in Christ, is the basis for wholesome life together.

Before the Session

Read Session 1 and the assigned Bible passage. Gather enough paper and pencils for each participant to use during the "Claim Your Story" discussion.

Claim Your Story

Begin by reading the first two paragraphs of the "Claim Your Story" section to the group. Then hand out paper and pencils and ask participants to respond to the question that begins the session—"Who tells you who you are?"—and also to "How do those persons or institutions label you?" Invite participants to share their answers to both questions.

Next, read the third paragraph to the group and ask if participants agree with the idea that when we join the church, it's the Lord who tells us who we are.

Ask: Which of those voices are you listening to when claiming your identity? Encourage people to answer based on their actual experience. While probably few will disagree that we should be listening to God, in reality, at different times and under various circumstances, we may be taking our primary identity from another voice. The point of encouraging the "in reality" answer is that our interaction with the Scriptures is not just to provide us with knowledge about the Corinthian letters but also to help us see where the Scriptures touch our lives and hearts and what they motivate us to do as a result.

Enter the Bible Story

Introduction

Ask how many participants have seen the movie *Remember the Titans*. Encourage those who recall the movie to tell the key point they remember from it. If no one is able to do so, narrate the brief outline of the story, as described in the first two paragraphs of the "Enter the Bible Story" section of the study.

Then explain Paul's concern about factions and lack of unity in Corinth.

Why is this concern still with the church today?

The City of Corinth

The material in this section helps us understand the context in which the Corinthian church existed and how that context pressured the church to be something other than what the gospel called it to be. Ask a volunteer to read the material in this section to the group.

What outside forces are pressuring the church today to be something other than what the gospel calls it to be?

The Three Letters to the Corinthians

This material is introductory to the Corinthian letters in general. If time is short, this can be omitted from discussion now. Otherwise, simply refer participants to it as background information. It will be covered in more detail in Session 5.

Letters in the Ancient World (1 Corinthians 1:1-9)

The twin themes introduced in this section are calling and fellowship. How do these themes define church membership today? How is each one expressed in your church?

Naming the Divisions in the Church (1 Corinthians 1:10-17)

A group from the Corinthian church brought Paul news about divisions there, with groups identifying themselves according to which preacher they followed: Paul, Apollos, or Cephas. Even those who self-identified as followers of Christ without naming a preacher where acting in a factional way.

In verse 13, Paul asked three questions. Read the questions to your group, and ask them how they would answer if they were Corinthians. How do you think the questions made them feel?

Christ the Power and Wisdom of God (1 Corinthians 1:18-31)

In what ways has following Jesus made him the center of your life? What things do you need to change to open the center of your life to Jesus?

What does it mean to say the foolishness of God is the heart of God's wisdom?

Proclaiming Christ Crucified (1 Corinthians 2:1-5)

Paul was criticized for not being a talented preacher, but he admitted his limitations. The writer suggests that our sense of ambition and competition may be our best tool for understanding the forces at work in the Corinthian congregation. Why might that be so?

The Wisdom of God (1 Corinthians 2:6-16)

Read the hymn in verses 5-11 to the group. In what ways does it function as a model for our lives?

The Danger of Divisions (1 Corinthians 3)

What Christian leaders helped you come to faith? What helped you continue in the faith when that leader was no longer available to you? What are the dangers of tagging your faith too closely to any single leader?

The Ministry of the Apostles (1 Corinthians 4:1-13)

Paul told the Corinthians that the role of the faithful is not to judge the work of God's servants but to take what has been given and be good stewards. What is the difference between holding people accountable and judging them?

With a Parent's Heart (1 Corinthians 4:14-21)

Paul had a parental interest in the Corinthians. Is this a good quality for a religious leader? Why or why not?

Live the Story

Ask participants to respond to the questions posed by the writer in the "Live the Story" section. Especially ask them to answer the final question, if not out loud, at least in their hearts.

Close with prayer, asking God to help each person to find not only a personal answer to that question, but also the determination to act on it.

2. Where the World Stops and the Church Begins
1 Corinthians 5–11

Faith Focus

The Christian life shows itself in specific conduct within the church, which makes life together a blessing to all within the faith community.

Before the Session

In this session, the writer uses the phrase *the world* to denote the environment outside of the church that recognizes neither the claims of God nor the Lordship of Christ. While some participants may immediately understand the phrase that way, others may not, so be prepared to define *the world* as it's used in this context. Think of what other words could be synonyms for the world.

Claim Your Story

With the group, use the instructions in the "Claim Your Story" section about considering your church building and your congregation's worship. Ask participants to answer aloud the questions posed in this section by the writer. Then ask: How does what you see, hear, and do in worship affect what you do as a result of worship?

Enter the Bible Story

Sexual Immorality in the Church (1 Corinthians 5)

The writer explains a situation of sexual immorality involving a member of the Corinthian church and directs the congregation to expel the accused man. The man's behavior was not unheard of in the city of Corinth, but it was not acceptable in the church. Paul's concern was that if the church does not distinguish itself from the world, no one will be able to tell where the world stops and the church begins.

Where is the world's agenda luring the church today? How should the church respond? Should the church do more "loving and structured dialogue" with participants who engage in behavior unacceptable in the church? Why or why not?

Lawsuits Among Believers (1 Corinthians 6:1-11)

Paul viewed lawsuits among believers as another example of the Corinthians letting the world set the agenda for the church.

Ask a volunteer to read verses 7-8. Is it better to be defrauded, as Paul suggested, than to be defeated in the faith by the world?

Participants of Christ (1 Corinthians 6:12-20)

Read verses 12-20 to the group. What does Paul mean by "freedom" in verse 12? What is the logic of Paul's argument in verses 15-16? What things do you do differently from how you might otherwise because your body is a temple of the Holy Spirit? (verses 19-20).

Marriage, Celibacy, Divorce, and Remarriage (1 Corinthians 7)

Because Paul thought that Christ was going to return soon, he viewed issues around marriage as of secondary importance. As a realist, however, he gave advice for how Christians should handle marriage matters in the meantime.

How might the fact that Christ has not yet returned change Paul's advice today? What is the principle behind his advice? Does that principle still fit Christians?

Meat Offered to Idols (1 Corinthians 8)

Few people today will identify with Paul's discussion about meat offered to idols, as there is no exact equivalent of this in our society today. However, what other kinds of things that are harmless in themselves ought Christians avoid because they might result in the downfall of a weaker Christian?

Privileges of an Apostle (1 Corinthians 9:1-18)

The matter of financial support for Christian leaders and the church's missions comes up in this section. To what degree is supporting missions a matter of necessity for Christians? Assuming people have sufficient income, is it possible for them to be committed Christians while not financially supporting the work of the church? Why or why not?

Discipline of Christian Freedom (1 Corinthians 9:19-27)

What is the difference between "freedom from" and "free for"?

Read Paul's words about self-discipline in verses 24-27. How do flexibility and self-discipline work together in the life of faith?

Christian Freedom and Moral Obligation (1 Corinthians 10:1–11:1)

Ask a volunteer to read aloud 10:23. To what degree do you agree with Paul's comment there?

Read 11:1 aloud. What does it mean to be "Christ-like"? Is that possible?

Questions Concerning Christian Worship (1 Corinthians 11:2-34)

This section addresses decorum in worship and while celebrating the Lord's Supper. The writer points out that the specifics of those things applied to Paul's day; they apply in our day in principle only. What is the principle behind Paul's advice on these matters? In what ways do we pass that principle on to younger generations of churchgoers?

Live the Story

The writer points out that of necessity, most of us spend a lot more time in the world than we do in the church. The writer then asks, "How are we supposed to resist being completely submerged in the values of the world when we are there most of the time?" How indeed? Ask participants to assume that a new Christian has asked them that question. What responses might they give?

Next, ask your group to consider the other questions posed in this section.

Finally, invite participants to stand in a circle and join hands. Let as many as wish to do so to offer sentence prayers for your congregation. Conclude the prayer by saying, "Hear our prayers, O Lord; in the name of Jesus. Amen."

3. The Gifts of the Spirit
1 Corinthians 12–14

Faith Focus
A healthy life together in the faith community depends not only on Christ, the head, but also on individual believers and the exercise of their gifts for the good of the body.

Before the Session
Read Session 3 and the assigned passage from 1 Corinthians. Secure a markerboard or a large sheet of paper and markers for use in the session.

Claim Your Story
The writer says that while there are times when a spirit of competition can be exhilarating and can develop one's personal strength and endurance, that spirit does not translate into every endeavor. In many settings, including the church, a spirit of cooperation is more appropriate and more helpful.

On a markerboard or a large sheet of paper, make two columns, one headed "Spirit of Competition" and one headed "Spirit of Cooperation." Then ask participants to think of as many human endeavors as they can and decide which column each belongs in. Here are a few to get you started: sports, civic clubs, hunting, preparing dinner, doing good deeds, driving, gardening, hobbies, worshiping God, shopping.

Next, read the last two paragraphs of the "Claim Your Story" section of the study. Ask participants to respond to the two questions in the last paragraph.

Enter the Bible Story
Introduction
This section sets the stage for the rest of the "Enter the Bible Story" discussion. Read this section to your group.

Remind your group that *spiritual gifts* are talents and abilities given to us by God to be used for the common good. Tell the group that one common definition of a *spiritual gift* is that it is something that a person can do well and is something that he or she enjoys doing.

Most of us have things we can do well if we have to, but we do not enjoy doing them.

Likewise, most of us have things we enjoy doing but aren't especially good at. Do you think God would ask us to offer most of our service through work that we detest or have no talent for? Why or why not?

Name one ability at which you are proficient and that you enjoy. Have you made this gift available to the church? Why or why not?

The Gifts of the Spirit (1 Corinthians 12)

Most of Paul's discussion in Chapter 12 is based on his comparison of the church, the "body of Christ," to the human body. Paul insisted that all parts are important. Assuming all of your body parts are healthy and functioning properly, which part, if eliminated, would make your body more efficient?

Why is the person who practices the gift of hospitality in the church kitchen just as important to the church as the person who preaches the sermons or leads the choir or diapers babies in the nursery?

Why isn't it usually a church goal to have a congregation full of people with high-profile gifts?

The Primacy of Love (1 Corinthians 13)

Most people are at least somewhat familiar with 1 Corinthians 13, if only from hearing it read at weddings. However, Paul wrote it as part of his discussion about spiritual gifts.

Paul started by mentioning "tongues," the gift some members of the Corinthian church possessed that enabled them to erupt in praise of God but in an unknown language. If anyone in your group has experienced or witnessed tongues, have that person describe what that means personally, from a spiritual viewpoint. How does it function in the worshiping community? Apparently some of the Corinthians with this gift thought, because it was a high-profile expression of praise, that it was a superior gift. Is the gift of tongues viewed that way today? Why or why not?

Paul argued that faith, hope, and love are the highest calling of all Christians. Of those three, he says that love is the greatest. Why do you think he narrowed down to those three and then to that one?

Speaking in Tongues (1 Corinthians 14)

Echoing Paul's thought in 1 Corinthians 14, the study writer says, "While speaking in tongues can contribute to disunity of the church, the gift of prophecy contributes to its unity. Speaking in tongues advances the individual, where prophecy advances the entire congregation." Why would that be so?

Paul offered three tests for evaluating how tongues should function in the church. The study writer has outlined and explained them. Ask participants to think of one of their own spiritual gifts and evaluate it in light of these three tests. Then ask any who are willing to share what they discovered by doing so.

Live the Story

The "Live the Story" questions in the study are designed to help participants identify their own gifts and make them available to the church. Point participants to the partial list of gifts Paul gives in 1 Corinthians 12:7-10, 28. Then ask them to name other gifts that should be added. List these on a markerboard or a large sheet of paper.

Next, ask participants to consider and discuss the questions in the "Live the Story" section. Finally, ask for someone who has the gift of praying to close the session with prayer.

4. Hope Really Does Float
1 Corinthians 15–16

Faith Focus

Jesus Christ's "first crop" resurrection affirms that resurrection will come to all who live and die in the faith community and is what animates life together in the community.

Before the Session

Read Session 4 and the assigned passage from 1 Corinthians.

Take a few moments to think about your view of the resurrection of believers. Some Christians are focused on living their lives in such a way as to gain eternal life. Other Christians, while not discounting resurrection, focus more on the meaning of faith in the present circumstances. The first group may be more animated and motivated by the hope of the resurrection than the second group, but that is not to say that either group is wrong. People are drawn to the different aspects of the Christian faith.

Nonetheless, the resurrection of Jesus and the resurrection of the faithful are the subjects of this session; and you will likely find it helpful to have thought beforehand about what it means to you.

Claim Your Story

In this section, the writer says that the opposite of faith is not doubt, but hopelessness. Doubt, he says, "is a common experience among all believers" and is provoked by personal growth.

Since personal growth happens in stages, it's not uncommon for believers to go through more than one period of doubt. How often has that happened to you? How was your faith different after an extended time of wrestling with doubt?

Why would the opposite of faith be not doubt, but hopelessness? What yanks you toward despair? How does faith help to pull you away from despair? How does your understanding of resurrection figure into that?

Enter the Bible Story

Introduction

This section is an introduction to the whole session. Ask a volunteer to read it aloud to the group.

The Historical Tradition (1 Corinthians 15:1-11)

Paul mentioned many people who saw the resurrected Jesus. All of these witnesses are now dead, of course, but in what way does the record of what they saw help in your understanding of the Resurrection?

The Importance of the Resurrection (1 Corinthians 15:12-19)

Some Corinthians questioned whether there would be general resurrection of all believers. Do you think this was evidence of a lack of faith? of personal growth? of hopelessness? Why?

The Order of Events (1 Corinthians 15:20-28)

Paul suggested an order of how the resurrection will be played out in the world. Jesus was the "first crop." The second crop comprises those who belong to Christ at his coming, and the rest is the general resurrection when Christ hands over the kingdom to God the Father.

In this line of thought, one meaning of Christ's resurrection is that it sets the pattern and proves the reality of resurrection. In what way is this meaningful to you? How does this help you in your life? How does it help when you are confronted by the death of loved ones?

Baptism for the Dead (1 Corinthians 15:29-34)

Read this section from the study book to the group. Ask: In what ways was your baptism an expression of confidence in the promise of resurrection? In what ways does it continue to be?

The Resurrection of the Body (1 Corinthians 15:35-58)

Paul attempts to answer questions about how resurrection happens and what is the nature of the resurrected body by using the analogy of a seed that "dies" when planted in the ground but then emerges as fruit. However, when Paul's explanation moves to the defeat of death, he seems to say that the whole matter of resurrection is a mystery. The study writer adds that that may be the best explanation we have.

Are you comfortable with mystery as part of your faith? Why or why not? Can something be a mystery and comforting at the same time? How does mystery help keep hope afloat?

Concluding Exhortation and Personal Matters (1 Corinthians 16)

This section introduces the next three. Read it to your group.

Collection for the Saints (1 Corinthians 16:1-4)

Ask: Do you find it easier to raise money for local church projects than to meet needs far from home? What motivates you to give to far away projects among people you don't know? Is it important from a spiritual perspective to contribute to such offerings? Explain your answer.

Plans for Travel (1 Corinthians 16:5-12)

Paul indicated that he hoped eventually to come to Corinth for a visit, and he seemed to imply that the Corinthians should deal with the problems he had addressed in the letter. Apollos, another preacher that some Corinthians had tried to rally around, had decided, probably for the good of the church, to not visit Corinth at that time.

Ask: When, for the good of the church fellowship, is absence the right thing to do?

Greeting and Benediction (1 Corinthians 16:13-24)

Along with his final greetings, Paul reminded the Corinthians to stand firm in their faith, stay strong and do everything in love. In what ways can we convey such encouragement to our fellow worshipers?

Live the Story

Ask participants to consider the questions in the "Live the Story" section and discuss their answers.

Ask: What does this session motivate you to do differently in your life of faith?

Close with prayer, asking God to help each participant find their faith expanding as they undergo personal growth.

5. When a Tough but Truthful Word Is Needed
2 Corinthians 10–13

Faith Focus
Life together in the faith community and its continuing vitality and health require speaking the truth in love.

Before the Session
Read Session 5 and the assigned passage from 2 Corinthians. You will notice that the assigned reading for this session skips the first nine chapters of 2 Corinthians, which are deferred to Session 6. The study explains the reason for this; but take the time to read that section carefully, as well as the comments about that section in this Leader's Guide, to be sure you understand the "three-letter theory."

Claim Your Story
Invite participants to share experiences where someone has confronted them about an attitude or behavior, speaking a truth that was difficult to listen to about themselves, but which was presented in such a way that the confrontation was an act of love.

What is the difference between "speaking the truth" and "speaking the truth in love"?

Where are the boundaries for Christians when confronting someone about inappropriate or destructive behavior?

Enter the Bible Story

The Three-Letter Theory
Read this section to the group. Discuss it only if there are any questions.

It's possible that someone in your group may object to assuming the last four chapters preceded the first nine, thinking this "tinkers" with the Word of God.

One way to respond is to point out that when our ancestors in the church gathered the letters of Paul for inclusion in the New Testament, they considered them all so valuable that they did not want to omit even a word, not even when the tone of one portion did not seem to match the tone of what preceded it.

It is possible, of course, that Chapters 10–13 comprise a later letter to the Corinthians, but that would assume that the mended relationship with the Corinthians had deteriorated yet again. The three-letter theory as described in the study is plausible and explains the information found in the texts of 1 and 2 Corinthians.

Paul Defends His Ministry (2 Corinthians 10:1-18)

Without understanding the context in Corinth, it is easy to see Paul as a braggart about his accomplishments on behalf of the gospel. However, the context makes a difference; and Paul needed to tout what he had done so that his teachings in the current dispute were taken seriously.

When have you thought it necessary to enumerate your accomplishments? Did it help? Why or why not?

Paul's Assessment of the "Super Apostles"(2 Corinthians 11:1-15)

Paul had to defend himself and his ministry against critics he called "super apostles."

Ask a volunteer to read to the group the last two paragraphs in this section. Ask people to comment on this statement from the writer: "Simply because we tell the truth, even in love, does not mean people want to hear." If the outcome of telling the truth in love is likely to be not accepted by the confronted person, should it be done anyway? What are the risks of not doing the truth-telling?

Paul's Apostolic Suffering (2 Corinthians 11:16-33)

Read 2 Corinthians 11:23b-28 to the group (starting with "I've been imprisoned . . ."). Paul was not bragging for bragging's sake, but he was pointing to his suffering to assert his authenticity as an apostle.

Ask a volunteer to read aloud the last paragraph in this section of the study. About what concerns have you experienced similar intensity? In what ways do you put your passion to work for the Lord?

Visions and Revelations of the Lord (2 Corinthians 12:1-13)

Although he told it in third person, Paul used personal testimony (verses 1-5) to authenticate his message. What is your testimony about Christ? Where have you had the opportunity to share it? What was the outcome?

Paul Anticipates a Third Visit to Corinth (2 Corinthians 12:14–13:10)

Paul summed up his arguments and spoke plainly, confronting the Corinthians with hard but necessary truth. Ask participants to read silently 12:19–13:2. What phrases indicate that Paul was telling the truth in love? In what ways does Paul's truth-telling in these verses serve as a model for how you might confront someone in the church who is behaving badly? Where might you use a different but still truthful approach?

Farewell (2 Corinthians 13:11-13)
Read this section of the study to the group.

Live the Story

Invite the group to answer each of the questions in the "Live the Story" section of the study.

Remind everyone that the Faith Focus Statement for this session is "Life together in the faith community and its continuing vitality and health require speaking the truth in love." Then ask participants to stand in circle. Invite as many are willing to offer a sentence prayer, thinking about the vitality and health of your church. Conclude the prayer time with your own prayer, asking God to help each one present with both courage and wisdom for those times when he or she needs to confront someone in truth and love.

6. Mending Our Relationships

2 Corinthians 1–9

Faith Focus

Reconciliation is what repairs the faith community and restores the health of the life together.

Before the Session

Read Session 6 and the assigned passage from 2 Corinthians. Gather a markerboard or a large sheet of paper and markers for use in group.

Claim Your Story

On a markerboard or a large sheet of paper, make three columns. Head the first one "Offense," the second one "Forgive," and the third one "Forget." Ask participants to tell of some times when someone has hurt them or they have hurt someone else. Write each of the offenses participants name in the first column. Then, for each offense, ask what forgiving the offender would look like. Write that answer in the "Forgive" column. Then ask what forgetting that offense would look like. (Mention that while we usually cannot actually forget, we can act as though the offense is forgotten.) Here are a couple of examples to get you started:

Offense	Forgive	Forget
Telling your personal secret to others. The person has since apologized to you.	Saying, "I am hurt that you did that, but I will not hold it against you. I still count you as a friend."	Never mentioning the offense again
Your teenager steals money from your purse. Later admits it and asks for forgiveness.	Explaining how such actions damage trust, but then saying, "I accept your apology, and I do forgive you.	Letting go of anger over the offense.

Read the last paragraph of the "Claim Your Story" section of the study to your group.

Enter the Bible Story
Greeting and Thanksgiving (2 Corinthians 1:1-11)

Remind the group of the three-letter theory of the Corinthian correspondence, as explained in Session 5. According to that theory, the first nine chapters of 2 Corinthians are the "letter of reconciliation," aimed at restoring the relationship between Paul and the Corinthian Christians.

Paul Sincere in His Actions (2 Corinthians 1:12–2:4)

Paul explained that he had written the "painful letter" instead of coming in person, fearing that a face-to-face meeting under the circumstances might have escalated the conflict.

When have you written an apology note that helped to heal a rift? When have you written an angry letter but then not sent it? How did that help you? Did it keep things from getting worse?

Treatment of the Offender (2 Corinthians 2:5-11)

Paul instructs the Corinthians about continuing to deal with a person who has been disciplined by the congregation. Failure to forgive, says Paul, provides an opening for Satan. In what sense does refusing to forgive create an opening for our own spiritual deterioration?

Thanksgiving for God's Leading (2 Corinthians 2:12-17)

Read verses 14-16a to the group. What is the meaning of *aroma* and *smell* as Paul uses those words in this passage?

Ministries of the Old and New Covenant (2 Corinthians 3:1–4:6)

Paul's descriptions of the old and new covenants are not easy to understand but the study offers a helpful interpretation. Starting with paragraph four of this section of the study ("Using the language of 'new covenant' ...") and continuing to the end of this section, read the material to the group.

If Christians are under the new covenant, how does the old covenant help our faith and daily living?

Suffering, Power, and Hope of an Apostle (2 Corinthians 4:7–5:10)

Paul used the imagery of clay pots and tents to symbolize the fragility of the human body in which the gospel dwells. In what ways do your mortality and human weakness validate the gospel?